SACRAMENTO PUBLIC LIBRARY
828 "I" STREET
SACRAMENTO, CA 95814

11/2015

D1009072

Three Points of Contact

Three Points of Contact

12.5 Ways to Jumpstart your Life and Weather Any Storm

Gregory Q. Cheek

Three Points of Contact
12.5 Ways to Jumpstart Your Life and Weather Any Storm
© 2015 Gregory Q. Cheek

All rights reserved. This book or any portion thereof may not be reproduced, distributed, or transmitted in any form or by any other means, including photocopying, recording, or other electronic or mechanical methods, without the express written permission of the publisher except for the use of brief quotations embodied in critical reviews, book reviews, and certain other noncommercial uses permitted by copyright law.

Printed in the United States of America
Formatted and edited by Kristen Corrects, Inc.
Second proofread by Gillian Burgess
Cover art design by Rade Rokvic
Cartoons by Hannah Nyangoma Giesekus
Author Portrait by Jay Greene Photography

First edition published 2015
10 9 8 7 6 5 4 3 2 1

Cheek, Gregory Q.
www.gregcheekspeaks.com
Three points of contact: 12.5 ways to jumpstart your life and weather any storm / Gregory Q. Cheek

ISBN-13: 9780692347027   paperback
ISBN-10: 069234702X   paperback
ISBN: 978-0-9863598-1-1   e-book
Library of Congress Control Number: 2015905652
Greg Cheek, Kansas City, MO
Interior Design by:
Kristen House of Kristen Corrects, Inc.

In an effort to support local communities, raise awareness and funds, a percentage of all book sales of this book will be presented to the following two organizations:

The University of Kansas Cancer Center Department of Radiation Oncology, Otolaryngology and the Head and Neck Support Group (SPOHNC).
Desert Manna, a Barstow, California-based nonprofit organization that provides housing, food, and alternative opportunities to homeless and disadvantaged individuals.

Get involved today
www.desertmanna.com or www.kucancercenter.org

Storms are a way of life! You don't have to outrun a storm.
Act Now!
Be properly prepared and make the storm work for you!

Table of Contents

To my mother and my hero!
Thanks for instilling an abundance of optimism into me every
day of my life

Erik, Nicole, and Stefanie
Live with perpetual optimism, maintain crystal-clear vision,
and always act on your instincts

Prologue

Ground Zero

The lowest moment of my life—two weeks removed from eight weeks of radiation and chemotherapy. The members of the Head and Neck Cancer Support Group at the University of Kansas Cancer Center hinted that the last couple of weeks after treatment would be the toughest. I thought the members of our support group were just exaggerating.

I was ready for this—at least I thought I was. POW!

My throat was completely closed and sealed after the third week of treatment. The discomfort intensified and the Fentanyl patch was losing its edge to hold back the raging pain in my body. I had no energy and was rapidly losing weight. The phlegm in my throat backed up more and more, and I was vomiting bile and blood from my empty stomach a couple times each hour.

I'd lost the momentum and initiative that I had worked so hard to build over the previous ten weeks. I slept on the bathroom floor for three straight days and had just enough energy to vomit in a paper towel, lift my arm up, and push it over the top into the toilet.

I lay back against the cool shower wall and looked outside the small second-floor bathroom window into the dark and cloudy Missouri night. My breath became shallow, and I could see a radiant light in the distance. The light got closer and closer before I suddenly... dozed off.

We all find ourselves either entering, in the middle of, or leaving some kind of storm. Like a soldier's compass, the enclosed lessons in the *Three Points of Contact: 12.5 Ways to Jumpstart Your Life* have guided me through every storm imaginable. They are all tried and tested in the toughest of times. May they bring you all the success and happiness you desire!

Introduction

My Initial Three Points Scenario
Listen to Yourself and Maintain Three Points of
Contact

At
All Times!

"Best case scenario for you—and I wish I had better news—they will likely cut your tongue out, and you will sit on some beach until you die." The voice, coming from my cell phone, beamed with arrogance.

This was the first and last time I accepted any medical advice outside of my medical team. Earlier that day, I went through my first day of in-processing and initial assessments of my cancer diagnosis. My mind was anesthetized from a day full of poking, biopsies, sticking, and scanning. I had a quick initial meeting with the members of my medical team from the University of Kansas Cancer Center, led by Dr. Lisa Shnayder, my surgeon and the best head and neck cancer doctor in the world. The professionalism of the entire team was impressive and noteworthy throughout the long day of evaluations.

The tumor board is a star chamber of cancer experts tasked with assessing my diagnosis and establishing viable treatment courses of action for my case. My entire life and future would be decided in the next forty-eight hours.

I sat in a restaurant parking lot on a warm, breezy evening in Kansas City, Missouri and could not shake the "best scenario" call of sitting on the beach with no tongue, waiting to die. At this point, nobody had explained to me what stage III head and neck cancer really meant. The facial expressions of my medical staff during the initial evaluation were mixed with professional confidence and obvious concern. The non-verbal feedback throughout the day clearly reflected that this would be a tough situation.

I drove to the backside of Kansas City International Airport off I-29. This location was a perfect perch to watch planes take off and land. This location became my intermittent "happy place" after my diagnosis. I thought of all my travels and happier times in my life as I watched the first plane roar overhead. I thought again about the phone call from the so-called cancer expert who supposedly researched thousands of cancer cases. According to several local cancer survivors, this gentleman was an extremely reliable source outside WebMD for a best-case prognosis. Then, as I stared at a blank page in my journal, it hit me. The Three Points of Contact immediately kicked in just as the second plane crossed overhead and landed on the other side of the fence line.

Optimism!

Optimism is the first point of contact—the optimistic trigger automatically takes control whenever you hear any negativity. The glass can be a hundred percent empty, and the optimistic person will find a drop of positivity on the brim of the glass.

For the next two to three minutes, I brainstormed like crazy in my journal all the existing optimistic possibilities. I immediately prioritized them from most to least important. Amazing, the clarity you discover when you focus solely on optimistic opportunities and positivity. The optimistic person will find the positives even in the darkest and most troubling of times!

My list of priorities immediately formed a clear #1 and #2 reasons to be optimistic right now.

When I was diagnosed with cancer, I'd been talking about (1) *writing a book* and (2) *starting a speaking business* for fifteen years. This is my dream and my life's passion! I'd worked three jobs simultaneously for the last seventeen years, yet never pursued these dreams.

No matter how many times I listened to Steve Jobs' famous 2005 "Connect the Dots" presentation at Stanford University, I kept putting the book and speaking business off until "someday." Now is the time to become the entrepreneur I dreamed of!

Once your priorities are straight, it's time to transition to the second point of contact.

Visualization!

Visualization kicks in once you have a clear and prioritized list. I got out of the car and lay on the hood as the third plane flew overhead. I closed my eyes as the warm breeze swayed across my body, then meditated for ninety solid minutes. Absolutely no thought about cancer, illness, death, or that dreadful phone conversation. Absolute crystal-clear visualization on the future success of my book and speaking business.

I slid off the hood with a rush of enthusiasm and gazed at the stream of cars buzzing north and south on Interstate 29 behind me. With the visualization complete, it was time to transition to the third point of contact.

Action!

Action is the execution step of this process—and there's no turning back.

It's a hundred percent all the way!

I sat back in the car and spent the next two hours writing my action plan in my journal. At this point, I was filled with massive enthusiasm and optimism, and visualized the book down to the last page number. My strategic action plan was now completely written in my journal.

In my mind, I was now cancer-free and ready to achieve my dream now! The Three Points of Contact were created to maintain balance in an ever-changing and challenging world.

No turning back. Perfect trifecta of the Three Points of Contact.

The ability to maintain these three points in unison—like a tripod—is critical to your success. The 12.5 methods were developed over the course of my lifetime and fit within these Three Points of Contact.

Bottom Line Up Front (BLUF)

It's not over until you achieve your dreams
Cancer hates happiness
Cancer never wins
It's not over until you win
Life's problems hate happiness too
Live with unrelenting optimism, crystal-clear vision of your
dreams, and act first
Live every moment of your life with enthusiasm
I believe in YOU!

The "Most Important Tool" as You Read this Book: Your Personal Journal/Notebook

I keep a journal, and every day I write down one great play that I had that day. I don't write down any negatives.
HEATHER O'REILLY, USA SOCCER SUPERSTAR

You will find a journal or notebook will help immensely as you embark on the journey into the Three Points of Contact. The Three Points of Contact utilizes note taking as a key mechanism for everything including personal reflection, chapter action activities, and goal setting. I hope you get into the habit of carrying the journal with you everywhere as you move up the ladder of success and achieve all your dreams.

Pre-Launch Briefing

Now that we viewed a mini "real world" scenario of the Three Points of Contact and have our journal, I'd like to introduce you to my mindset, an initial definition of each of the three points, the twelve chapters, and chapter 12.5: Live Every Day with Enthusiasm.

The First Point of Contact

Optimism

> *One of the most significant findings in psychology in the last twenty years is that individuals can change the way they think.*

Dr. Martin Seligman, *Learned Optimism*

Your chances of living a life of with an abundance of health, happiness, and success will increase exponentially when you develop the traits of an optimist. This first point of contact is extremely critical for everyone from the pessimist to a fully optimistic person.

The quote above stems from one of the biggest breakthroughs ever in the history of positive psychology. Until the mid-1960s, the scientific community argued that optimistic and pessimistic behaviors were a result of our conditioning and shaped the way we show up, behave, and act. Dr. Martin Seligman tells us, "Life inflicts the same setbacks and tragedies on the optimist as the pessimist, but the optimist weathers them better. The optimist can bounce back from defeat over and over again. The pessimist gives up and falls into depression." Optimistic people achieve more at work, at school, in athletics, and are much healthier.

The chapter is created with my personal and rather unique way of showing how you can drastically improve your optimistic behavior. This first point of contact can completely change the behavior of the pessimist and provide new skills for the most talented optimist.

The first four chapters in this first point of contact were carefully crafted to provide you with an energized, optimistic viewpoint on life and everything around you. The tools in this chapter will prepare you to move to the next two points of contact and to chapter 12.5: Live Every Day with Enthusiasm.

1. ***You Must Be Relentless:*** Your golden key to becoming an optimist is becoming completely relentless. This chapter will show you how to turn setbacks, failure, and unfortunate events into temporary situations and not permanent ones. You will learn the valuable tools of becoming forever relentless and quickly bouncing back from life's struggles. It's never over until you win!

2. ***Manage Your Self-Talk:*** Perpetual and consistent optimism is a belief in yourself. Truly optimistic people know how to manage and control their thinking via positive self-talk. This chapter will show you how to master the use of controlling your thoughts through self-talk. You must stop all negative self-talk and maintain positive communication with yourself at all times.

3. ***Practice Karma Daily:*** You will learn to handle external distractions in your life with calmness and control. I will share with you the critical optimistic traits of quieting the mind, silencing yourself, and looking at the world through the successful eyes of the perpetual optimist, among other tools. This chapter is life changing.

4. ***Integrate Thanks into Your Daily Life:*** This extremely powerful chapter will change your life and simply turn giving thanks into a steering wheel to your optimism. Optimistic people are thankful people! This chapter shares all the physical, mental, and medical benefits of being thankful.

The Second Point of Contact
Visualization

> *Vision without action is merely a dream. Action without vision just passes the time. Vision with action can change the world.*
>
> Joel A. Barker

Upon completion of your full optimistic view on any situation, immediately turn to visualization.

Every success I ever achieved, I vividly pictured first.

If you cannot see it, you will have a more difficult time achieving it.

In a study documented at Vanderbilt University, visualization—like optimism—was defined as mental imagery or mental rehearsal. According to the study, the reason visual imagery works is that when you imagine yourself performing to perfection and doing precisely what you want, you are physiologically creating neural patterns in your brain, just as if you had physically performed the action.

Mental imagery works best if you visualize a set of sequential steps for a foolproof visualization process. There is no correct way to practice mental imagery—it's left up to your preferences and present circumstances. My visualization process differs before an interview, exam, workout, cancer treatment, marathon, work presentation, or every day before I started writing this book. The visualization process is situation independent.

The process and depth of visualization varies on the situation. Mental preparation for a marathon begins months before the race, while my visualization began just minutes prior to every radiation treatment.

5. ***Turn It All Off and Empty Your Cup:*** You can only begin to effectively visualize when you're able to empty all the thoughts in your head (cup). This chapter focuses on finding your stillness, locating your happy place, finding peace, bliss, and simply quieting the mind. The road to successful visualization starts in this chapter.

6. ***Be in the Top Three Percent Now:*** This chapter will describe the masterful art of goal setting. Your ability to set goals, take action, and follow through to become part of the top three percent will determine whether or not you live a successful life. This chapter will share with you my personal goal-setting mechanism. I've used this process to accomplish more goals in the last four years since my diagnosis than in the previous twenty years.

7. ***Establish Trust and Belief in Yourself:*** This chapter includes a tailored roadmap to assist you in establishing trust and belief in yourself. Happy, enthusiastic, successful, proactive, and energetic people have an innate ability to feel the law of belief or law of attraction—they also trust themselves and other people. Your satisfaction in your life, career, and relationships are all directly tied to trust. All relationships are built on trust. I believe in you and trust you! Let's do it!

8. ***Resilient as a Duffel Bag:*** I picked up the idea of the resilient duffel bag while living in Stuttgart, Germany. I live in the downtown market area of Sindelfingen and about 500 meters from the entrance to the largest Mercedes-Benz assembly plant in the world. I see hundreds of immigrants daily from all over Eastern Europe, the Mediterranean, and Africa. These people arrive with no resources, in many cases

cannot speak German, and have all their possessions in one single bag. I refer to the hiring point at the 30,000-employee Mercedes-Benz assembly plan as a modern-day Ellis Island. All their hopes and dreams left behind, they arrive here starting anew. I talk to them every day, and I admire their tenacity, optimism, and belief that life will get better as they all chance the unknown. Wow! I'm just in awe of their resilience. I will share in this chapter my unique combined lessons of my resilient life and those of the immigrants I've followed here in Germany for the past forty-two months. I'm so excited to help build your own resilient duffel bag for your life. Can you imagine the goals, success, and dreams you could achieve with your resources if you had the adventure, confidence, energy, and resilience of these tenacious people?

The Third Point of Contact

Action

> *Action is the foundational key to all success.*
>
> Pablo Picasso

This is the easiest and yet the most difficult of the Three Points of Contact. This is why so many people fail—they never get started. You must take action with unrelenting determination and live every day with enthusiasm in everything you do!

The key to action is you *must* take the first step! You must become a person of action!

Your ability to take decisive action is a direct correlation to your success. Hesitation, delay, and excuses will ultimately lead to failure. Take action now and believe in your vision.

The combination of enthusiasm, crystal-clear visualization, and confidence to take that first step will place you on the path to successful action. When you take your first step, you must have the attitude that you will not stop until you reach your destination.

But what if you begin to lose momentum or you see yourself losing concentration? Easy fix. Immediately go back to your visualization process and re-visualize again. And if the visualization is not working, you go back to optimism. Success will be defined when all three legs stand together in combination with massive enthusiasm.

The following four chapters were developed to assist you with taking and maintaining decisive action right now! For the rest of your life.

9   ***Make Plans to Travel Today:*** You will learn the benefit of travel and how it increases your ability to act in every other facet of your life. Learning to love and appreciate travel will change your life forever!

10. ***Carry Your Ruck at All Times:*** The freedom and ease of carrying your ruck will motivate you to take action today. Learn simple, easy, and exhilarating steps to taking impromptu action in your life.

11. ***Upgrade Your Personnel Healthcare Plan:*** Your health is linked directly to your positive behavior and willingness to jump out and take action. These simple suggestions and lessons will improve your health.

12. ***Communicate Like Your Life Depends on It!*** Action and communication are directly linked to one another. Your career, success, dreams, goals, and ability to take decisive action depend on your ability to communicate

effectively—your life does depend on this skill! Enjoy the unique way we mix critical skills that will provide the confidence to not only take action, but also motivate others.

I wish you all the best in using my Three Points of Contact. Please contact me if you have any comments or questions. I can't wait to hear from you!

Have an amazing Three Points of Contact day, and attack life with *enthusiastic action!*

Go get 'em!

Sincerely,

Greg Cheek

Three Points of Contact

"The Blueprint"

12.5

Live Every Day with Enthusiasm

*Enthusiasm is an amazing tool. When you show
enthusiasm and willingness to work hard, people
can't help but come run to help you succeed. Despite
everything in life, be super enthusiastic!*

Mike Jutan

I agonized for months over the placement of enthusiasm as I developed the content for this book. I've had a wonderful life using thirteen base values that make up the strategic system of the Three Points of Contact. Visualization and action were obvious choices for the second and third leg.

I was completely torn between the choices for the first leg. It was a draw between optimism and enthusiasm in the triangular support of my strategies and the Three Points of Contact. I looked closely at both characteristics throughout my life. After a complete examination of my life, it seems fitting that optimism is the first and most important leg.

The enthusiasm chapter is strategy 12.5 that covers each one of the three legs and all 12 methods. Thus, I named this chapter Live

Every Day with Enthusiasm. You simply can't have enthusiasm without optimism—at least I can't! If nothing else, be optimistically enthusiastic—that's a winner!

Successful people have a combined blend of enthusiasm and optimism. You must have a purpose in life, passion to live, always be seeking new opportunities, and have the ability to dream. You can Google *enthusiasm* and get a million different definitions and recommendations on how to improve your enthusiasm.

The Live Every Day with Enthusiasm chapter is located at the end of the book immediately after Chapter 12, Communicate Like Your Life Depends On It. This chapter will expand on all the areas I've used to get motivated, energized, and focused in order to maintain an enthusiastic purpose and mind state every day. I always carried the mantra that nobody can outwork yourself but you. That is true to a certain extent, but sometimes your work ethic is not enough. Just like the quote at the top of this chapter, enthusiasm is the great equalizer…and you must master this skill to achieve your full potential and reach your dreams.

OPTIMISM

OPTIMISM

OPTIMISM

Chapter One

You Must Be Relentless

Be relentless and you will break through.
Julie Brown

1

The Bathroom Floor

Determination becomes obsession and then it becomes all that matters.

Jeremy Irvine

I woke up at the end of the third day on the bathroom floor in the middle of the night. I had no energy to pull myself up anymore. I lay there for a minute, and I felt a warm wetness on the side of body. I looked down to my side—the fastener to my stomach Percutaneous Endoscopic Gastrostomy (PEG) feeding tube had dislodged and the liquid, bile, blood, and everything from my stomach was spread all over the floor. I laid my head on the ground, my ear in the moisture, and took a deep breath. I hadn't eaten in days, was severely dehydrated, and was falling into a depression. The moisture crept up my cheek, cool wetness rolling up my face and seeping into my right eye, and I didn't even care.

This is it—and for the only time in my entire life, for about five minutes, I quit!

The negative talk swarmed my head, and suddenly I became okay with the fact that I was going to die. I spoke to myself and began justifying my own demise. My defeatist self-talk was in full motion. My attitude was very clear in echoing that I've done the best I can, I've lived a good life, I've set a good example, and I've been a good person to others. I admit I made mistakes—but who doesn't? I'm all alone, and this is the way it is meant to end.

The words from my dentist, Dr. Lausten, rang in my head: "Greg, the sure killer with this cancer is not keeping up with nutrition." You must not get behind on your daily nutrition.

I lost the initiative, drive, desire, and visualization, and I somehow allowed myself to get acted upon. I closed my eyes and just thought, *Greg, you've got to come up with something. You can't quit now.*

I felt my breath start to falter and my heart rate slow to a crawl, and I could not raise my head off the floor. With one open eye and the other soaked in bile and fluids, I glanced through a crack in the bathroom door to a small table next to my desk. There was a picture of my daughter Nicole taken at her recent high school graduation. Nicole was just starting her freshman year as an engineering major at Seattle Pacific University.

My mind drifted to ten weeks earlier at the beginning of my chemotherapy and radiation treatment. Tears swelled and fell across my nose and cheek as I reminisced about the conversation with Chris Johnson, the head volleyball coach at Seattle Pacific University. Nicole had originally decided to go to college in California, but she called me on the first day of my chemotherapy treatment to tell me she changed her mind on her college location.

Nicole is an amazing student athlete and received a full academic and Army ROTC scholarship at the University of Washington. Nicole could pick any university that supported her engineering major and conducted ROTC through the University of Washington. I asked Nicole about volleyball, and she wasn't sure she would be able to find somewhere to play that late in the year—summer was nearing and the window on submitting college applications was closing.

A quick search on Google for the universities in the Seattle area brought up Seattle Pacific University. The beautiful private and academically strong Christian university is simply known in the northwest United States as SPU.

I called Coach Chris Johnson directly and spoke to him about the possibility of Nicole coming to play volleyball at SPU. Our discussion took place as the poisonous chemotherapy dripped in the IV in my right arm and my left arm was connected to the blood pressure cuff and several other monitoring devices. Coach Johnson agreed to take a chance on my seventeen-year-old daughter and opened a position for Nicole on the volleyball team. The University of Washington US Army ROTC program and Seattle Pacific University volleyball team worked out an agreement for Nicole to attend both universities.

The rest, as perfectly described within the Three Points of Contact, is a vision completed. Nicole just graduated from Seattle Pacific University with a bachelor's degree in engineering and is an active duty second lieutenant in the United States Army Engineer Corps.

As I lay on my bathroom floor back in Kansas City looking at that picture of Nicole, I kept telling myself, *C'mon, Greg! C'mon, Greg! You've been through tougher situations your entire life!*

I struggled to maintain a clear purposeful vision and told myself, *I want to watch Nicole play college volleyball, graduate college as an engineer, and get commissioned as a second lieutenant in the US Army.*

It seemed like yesterday when I slept on the front door mat at the local Air Force recruiting station. I was persistent—I stayed there until the recruiter enlisted me in the US Air Force. Nobody would have ever believed I could continue on and someday become a commissioned officer. College education was not discussed on my block and surely not in my house. Everyone I grew up with went to work immediately after finishing high school. Along with Nicole, my son Erik is finishing his college degree and is a staff sergeant in the US Air Force. My youngest Stefanie is a sophomore at California State University, Chico. The family tree has changed, and graduating from college has become an expectation—right on!

I lay there on the bathroom floor, the complete right side of my body soaked in my bodily fluids, tears streaming down my face.

My mind raced out of control as a trailer of all the past events in my life played: The long walk on my last day of high school to tell my mom that I had failed my civics class by a single point and would not graduate high school, living homeless behind a dumpster at the restaurant where I worked, sleeping on the ninth hole tee box bench at a local public golf course, and eventually curling up every night at the Air Force recruiter's doorstep.

I felt this pull of energy from the volleyball team at Seattle Pacific University—my intuition or the universe telling me to go see my daughter and the SPU volleyball team in San Francisco. That same universal pull I've felt my whole life, from leaving the house at eighteen to finding my freedom away from the nightmarish cancer thoughts when I started my practice at the Bikram Yoga Studio in Kansas City.

I glanced up at the window again and the light was gone.

I mustered every cancer-fighting white blood cell I had left, pulled myself on my side by the toilet stall, put my PEG tube fastener back on, and strapped the tube to the side of my stomach. I grabbed the sink and heaved myself up, standing on my wobbly legs. My reflection was frightening and startling—I had become a skeleton.

I stood up straight and struggled to maintain my balance even while leaning my thighs on the sink and placing both hands on the mirror. My legs shook and I looked hard at myself in the mirror and glanced again at the picture of Nicole. I stared back at myself in the mirror and said out loud,

"I'm going to make it to see Nicole become a second lieutenant, play college volleyball, graduate college, and become an engineer. I want to see what becomes of Erik and Stefanie."

Although I was a shadow of myself in the mirror, I stared as if to look through my eyes, through my soul as I softly said, "I'm relentless."

"I'm going to make it, because...I'm relentless and I'm not done living yet."

You Are Relentless

Becoming successful is a relentless pursuit. It's good that it's that way: When it does come, you learn to know how to appreciate it, and know how lucky you are to be doing something that you love so much.

Frankie Valli

Life is tough. You will get knocked around, and that's expected and that's okay. You will be better for it, and in the end, you become more and more relentless with these experiences.

Relentless is similar to the popular term *grind*. Sometimes you must put your head down and grind and keep grinding until you are through a situation. The word *relentless* has a more resounding effect, allowing various options and ideas to attack and continue attacking a problem for a long period of time. Relentless people have the ability to bounce back from every type of adversity.

You must be relentless to serve two-, three-, and four-plus one-year combat tours in the armed forces. Grinding will not get you through 365 days of working 24/7, in a job where your life could end at any second and you are thousands of miles away from your family and loved ones. This is an example of the need to encompass skills of resiliency. If you study success in various occupations from people all around the world, you will notice this similar characteristic of being relentless, striving for your dreams every day and never giving up.

Relentless is my sole being and characteristic, from the day I walked out of the house at eighteen years old with my rucksack into a world of the unknown. I didn't know where I was going, what I would do next, where I would stay each night. I decided that everything I do from here on would be with a hundred percent enthusiasm, desire, passion, focus, and I would be relentless for the rest of my life.

Make the decision right now—you will be relentless and never give up. You will achieve your goals and be successful by shaping your relentless behaviors every day.

Act or Be Acted Upon—Critical!

As soon as I became proactive in producing my own stuff, I started getting other roles.

Ray Liotta

This concept is so simple that it can sometimes be difficult to manage. You have a critical decision to make every day of your life. Do I approach life in a manner to act or get acted upon? Do I live life being proactive or reactive? If you don't prepare and act instead of always getting acted upon, life will act on you!

You must take the necessary action to prepare yourself for the future. Make it a habit to always act first! Just get into the mindset that I will take the initiative to prepare myself for the moment that life acts on me. Life will act on you, and you need to be ready!

In *The Seven Habits of Highly Effective People*, author Stephen Covey states that the difference between people who exercise initiative and those who don't is the difference between night and day:

> *I'm not talking about twenty-five to fifty percent dif-*
> *ference effectiveness;*
> *I'm talking about a five thousand percent difference,*
> *particularly if they are smart, aware, and sensitive to others.*

Initiative is key in living a productive, successful life. Take control of your life and *act today*!

Resilient Address of Hard Knocks – 5345 Madison Avenue

Was I always going to be here? No, I was not. I was going to be homeless at one time, a taxi driver, truck driver, or any kind of job that would get me a crust of bread. You never know what's going to happen.

Morgan Freeman

After talking to my best friend's father about his travels in the United States Air Force, I made a decision that I would go to the recruiting office and see about joining the Air Force. The recruiter, Technical Sergeant (TSgt) Daniels, boldly blocked me when he found out I didn't graduate high school with my class. He told me that my entrance scores were too low and I would be a risk to the Air Force for retainability; I should try another branch of the service.

This has been a theme in my life: Every time somebody puts a wall in front of me, I always figure out a way to go around or over the wall. This is again the difference between *grind* and *relentless*. I've grinded and I would just put my head down until I either gave up or was able to break though. Relentless people have the grinding sense, though they also look for alternate courses of action and attack with fierce action. I came and saw TSgt Daniels every day between my three jobs and asked him again and again about the Air Force. He would tell me I should see about the Army, the Navy, the Coast Guard, or the Marines. "I'm sorry; we can't use you at this time," he told me again and again.

Flash! I was being acted upon again. So I made the decision to act. Instead of sleeping behind the restaurant, in a truck, on the golf course, I decided I would just stay on this recruiter's doorstep at 5345 Madison Avenue in Sacramento until he had no choice but to take me in.

Initially TSgt Daniels gave me odd jobs—cleaning the recruiter car, cleaning the office, filing paper—and I came in every day showing enthusiasm, passion, and just saying over and over, "This is my dream, this is my dream, this really is my dream."

At the end of my second week of staying at the recruiter's doorstep, TSgt Daniels wanted to mail me some information about the possibility of getting into the Air Force at a later date. He asked me for my address; I told him I didn't have one, I was on my own. TSgt Daniels gave me the address at the doorstep I slept at until I received a "yes" to the U.S. Air Force.

"Okay, Cheek. You're not going anywhere and you have shown that you are motivated and enthusiastic," he said eventually. "Let's find something for you."

Two weeks later I departed and began my life journey to Lackland Air Force Base in San Antonio, Texas. I entered the United States Air Force with a home address of 5345 Madison Ave., the Air Force recruiter's office. My DD Form 214 still shows that address as entrance into the Air Force and is a source of pride for me.

By the way, to TSgt Daniels: Thanks for giving me my shot! I was not only motivated and enthusiastic, I was relentless! I've looked at that DD Form 214 since I departed the military service…and that keeps me motivated and proud of where I've come from!

Is There *Really* Always Tomorrow?

The best preparation for good work tomorrow is to do good work today.

Elbert Hubbard

No, there is not always tomorrow! Nobody is guaranteed tomorrow. I hear these words all the time: "I'll do something tomorrow." As a cancer survivor, I can give you a list of names of people who were here yesterday and are gone today.

You must live and act in today. There are times that my actions in being decisive for today have been successful, and there were others that were not so successful. I don't call these failures, I call them "not so successful attempts"—at least I took the chance and initiative to act and move out now!

One of my favorite habits in Covey's *Seven Habits* is the second one: begin with the end state in mind. You must focus and visualize on what your end state is going to be. You must focus today. If you wait until tomorrow—it may be too late.

I made the decision to leave the Air Force after my four-year commitment and go back to college. When I showed up at Shasta College in Northern California, I had a rucksack, $70 in my pocket, and the G.I. Bill for $225 a month. But the most valuable thing that I had in my ruck was the blank case from my high school diploma—blank because I never received my diploma when I failed that class my senior year.

That was my ultimate pictorial visualization: I visualized placing that associate's degree in that case twenty-four hours a day!

Throughout my college career, I again worked three jobs—as a resident advisor in the dorm and as a teaching assistant at the local school—and I remained in the United States Air Force Reserve, working one weekend a month and volunteering for any other additional duties as they became available. I visualized my bachelor's degree, and two years later, I slipped that into my case. I also visualized my master's degree and my eventual graduation from the United States Army Command and General Staff College.

I never realized how valuable that empty diploma case I carried all my life really was in maintaining my focus and relentlessness.

That is one relentless and very educated high school diploma case!

Action

Relentless piggy bank (RPB)

The RPB approach strengthens relentless behavior: Buy a piggy bank, and every time an adverse event occurs in which you are required to tolerate, overcome, and move forward positively, place money in the piggy bank. This works well when confronted by a colleague or friend who is especially difficult. Every time this colleague or friend acts in a threatening manner, put money into the piggy bank. At the end of a week or month, take the money out and spend it on something nice. This provides humor, a diversion from the threatening person, and ultimately pleasure. You may not be able to control the other person's response, but you can derive some "hidden" pleasure from their adverse behavior. You will see your tolerance and resilience begin to strengthen immediately.

The best defense is a good offense

Is the best defense a good offense? This is just another way of saying you can act or be acted upon. You have two choices in life. You can act and be the offense, or you can be acted upon and be the defense.

Keep a log in your journal for the next seven days. Draw a line down the center of the paper. On the top left of the paper, write *Act and Offense;* on the top right, write *Act Upon and Defense.* Leave a couple inches on the side of the paper so you can keep notes. You're going to keep score between the offense and defense.

Over the course of the each day, keep track of how many times you act upon something and how many times you are acted upon. Amazing how many times I caught myself in a situation that I needed to act before I was about to get acted upon! Because I subconsciously didn't realize I was in a position to go on the offense, I didn't. This technique has allowed me to improve significantly when it comes to acting on situations in my new speaking business.

Give this a shot for seven days. Write your comments on the side column, and send me a note and tell me what you think. Let me know if the old saying stands true: Is the best defense a good offense?

Key Points

- Be relentless; bounce back from life's struggles
- Decide daily: Act or be acted upon
- Be resilient—never give up
- Live and act in today
- Maintain focus

OPTIMISM

Chapter Two

Manage Your Self-Talk

What I'm looking for is not out there; it's in me.
Helen Keller

Notice When Negative Self-Talk Starts and Embrace Your Opportunities

4/06/2019

tem(s) Checked Out

ITLE   100 days of real food fast
BARCODE   33029102106663
DUE DATE   04-27-19

ITLE   Three points of contact :
BARCODE   33029066933052
DUE DATE   04-27-19

Thank you for visiting the library!
Sacramento Public Library
www.saclibrary.org

Love your library?
Join the Friends!
www.saclibfriends.org/join
Visit our Book Den, too.

Terminal #   24

side can hurt us.

AFRICAN PROVERB

ou and around you, and
journal the positive and
ne interaction at the mall,
al and national news sta-
to the unhappiness and
he lack of education, the
verything is unfair. You'll
is going on around us are

ative self-talk and invades
his negative self-talk when
nind immediately. Never,
! We only use about five

23

percent of our brain; unfortunately we fill that five percent with so much negativity all day long.

I love Stephen Covey's quotes on the positive mental attitude (PMA): "Smiling wins more friends than frowning," and "Whatever the mind of a man can conceive and believe, it can achieve." You must keep your mind directed toward positivity and the things you want. You are your own motivational speaker! Treat yourself the way you want others to treat you.

Cross out the negative talk you observed and focus on the beauty and positive flow of communication you experienced. Become accustomed to blocking out that negative talk. Write those feelings down; be precise, as we are looking for a pattern. What time is it? What type of music are you listening to? Who do you speak to? Who do you talk about? Why is it you feel this inner dialogue of positivity? This is the golden egg of maintaining positive self-talk.

Focus on what you want, not on what you don't want. Don't focus on fighting cancer—focus on being cancer-free. Don't focus on the three jobs you're working and the lack of sleep—focus on the graduation and the benefit at the end. Maintain a positive mental picture in your mind at all times. Prepare to post the Bulletin Board Material (BBM) we will discuss in a few pages.

You must constantly remind yourself that you are in complete control of the thoughts in your mind. You are the product of your thoughts; don't let others create your unhappiness or change your state of bliss. You are in charge of your own happiness. Follow your passion and enthusiasm every day.

My rule: You may be smarter than me, have more money than me, and come from some high-class family. However, you will never outwork me! I'm editing this at 3:00 AM and I need to catch the train in two hours to my daily opportunity and teach three college classes tonight—let's go!

Defend Your Schloss

If you hear a voice within you saying, "You are not a painter,"
then by all means paint and that voice will be silenced.

Vincent Van Gogh

Think of your mind as a castle—or a medieval *schloss* as they say in Germany. Close your eyes and imagine a schloss, many of which are still in place throughout Europe. The schloss is made of brick and mortar with strategically placed firing positions around the perimeter—and, of course, the ever-treacherous moat and drawbridge.

The only way you can enter the schloss is via the lowered drawbridge over the water. Unauthorized bridge access requires the adversary to swim across the water and climb over the wall (with the inhabitants of the castle, of course, having a field day from an optimal fighting position high on the wall—and not to mention what kind of unfriendly critters are floating in that water). Treat negative thoughts like the enemy trying to attack and enter the schloss. You are the king (*König*) high on the wall looking down at the thoughts trying to enter your schloss. You lower the drawbridge and allow only positive thoughts into your mind. You must treat negative thoughts as an enemy trying to invade your space in your schloss.

The schloss is secured twenty-four hours a day to ensure no entry. Entry into the schloss by the enemy of negative thoughts could be extremely harmful. Treat your mind the same way. Use the techniques found in this strategy to combat those negative thoughts and keep them not only outside the castle walls but also outside the moat. You will find that a schloss/mind filled with positive thoughts is the key to being on the road to three firm points of contact and focusing and attaining all your dreams. You are the *König* of your thoughts! Get up on the high wall and tell your soldiers when to raise and lower the drawbridge. Congratulations!

You are on your way to a schloss full of positivity and no negative self-talk.

Clean Your Hard Drive

Self-suggestion makes you master of yourself.

W. Clement Stone

Think of your mind as an external hard drive. We speak 140 to 180 words per minute, but we can listen to or store up to 700 to 800 words per minute. Your hard drive has plenty of open listening space for both the 20 percent positive self-talk and 80 percent negative self-talk you receive every day. You come equipped with the best negative self-talk anti-virus program in the world—use it! You must live with the talk on your hard drive and with the decisions you make. Align yourself with positive people—those who have the same goals as you and are striving for the top.

Keep your hard drive clean. Allow your positive friends to be your anti-virus to the negative talk. Listen to positive motivational speakers every day. Fill your hard drive with positive words and positive feedback.

Verbal Mantra and Bob Hope's Drill Sergeant

Once you replace negative thoughts with positive ones, you'll start having positive results.

Willie Nelson

Cyber self-talk is subconscious self-talk, the inner dialogue speaking to ourselves all the time. Although we guard our hard drives with positive friends, this is not enough. Our inner dialogue is constantly running—from the moment we get up in the morning and even during our sleep.

How do we stop this negative self-talk?

Here comes the drill sergeant in you! The military drill sergeant is a human version of a watchdog. You must use drill sergeant self-talk to get through your daily life. That drill sergeant is telling you to get up, get excited, and enjoy every day as if it were your last. No Negative Self-Talk!

As a youngster, I caddied at a local golf country club—Del Paso Country Club in northern Sacramento. I started caddying when I was thirteen years old. I would get on my trusted one-speed red Schwinn bicycle and ride to the other side of town to this exclusive country club. As I rode my bike in the early morning hours through a part of town that was not exactly safe at 4:00 AM, I repeated positive affirmations to myself. The thoughts of local fear and problems at home disappeared. I've used this technique my entire life.

The big reward for caddying all year was getting a prime caddie position for the annual Gene Littler Swing at Cancer Golf Tournament. I had the honor of caddying for some amazing people over the years including Johnny Miller, Andy North, Keith Fergus, Glenn Campbell, and my biggest thrill, for even the late, great Bob Hope. I was sixteen years old when I earned the right to caddie for Mr. Hope. We used a golf cart, as Mr. Hope had a difficult time walking.

We had lots of time to just sit and talk in the cart together. I noticed at one point early in the round that Mr. Hope was in a state of soft verbal self-talk. One of the most famous actors, entertainers, comedians, and impromptu speakers in the world was actually talking to himself!

I asked Mr. Hope, "Sir, is everything okay?" He smiled and said, "Yes, of course, I'm just talking to myself, I always talk to myself before I step up and address the golf ball. This gives me my own personal self-confidence before I hit the ball. I need all the help I can get in front of all these people. After all, I can't hit any worse that I'm hitting it now," he added with a chuckle and a pat on my back.

I asked as he walked away toward the massive gallery, "Mr. Hope, you do this all the time?"

"Absolutely, I owe everything I've accomplished to the ability to be my own personal drill sergeant through the use of self-talk."

It's not just me on my bike at 4:00 AM using self-talk, I realized. *Even the great Bob Hope does this...wow!*

I've used this type of motivational self-talk my entire life. I consider myself a motivational speaker, but I must first be a self-motivator. Much of my success and ability to self-motivate can be directly attributed to the words of wisdom that Mr. Bob Hope gave to a young sixteen-year-old with the easiest and most enjoyable life learning caddie loop I ever received.

Self-talk became second nature; I've had many instances in my life that I needed the self-talk, inner dialogue in order to support myself. I vaguely recall the words from the doctor after my surgical biopsy: "Greg, you have stage III cancer." I was speechless...but then I felt a virtual tap on the knee, as if I were sitting in the golf cart and sixteen again.

"Greg," Mr. Hope echoed in my mind, "I hope that drill sergeant is filling you up with positive self-talk thoughts about what you will do to celebrate when this is over."

I responded as I looked to the hospital ceiling. "Yes, sir, Mr. Hope, nothing but positive self-talk."

No Negative Thoughts— You Are Unstoppable!

If you want to reach a state of bliss, then go beyond your ego and the internal dialogue (self-talk). Make a decision to relinquish the need to control, the need to be approved, and the need to judge. Those are the three things the ego is doing all the time. It's very important to be aware of them every time they come up.

Deepak Chopra

My best friend Mike Nichols' mother used to tell us all the time, "You kids remember, no negative thoughts!"

I came from a household with lots of daily hardship situations. When I went to Mike's house, this was time to relax and leave all the negativity behind, even if only for a few hours. In my eyes, everything outside of my house seemed to be positive and wonderful. As I grew older, in using the following three techniques, I began to clearly understand the true meaning and wisdom of "no negative thoughts."

(1) *Recognize negative thoughts as they occur.* You must recognize that you're saying them to yourself. You don't realize how often these negative thoughts enter your subconscious. At times, we just accept everything that flows through our mind, whether it's good or bad, and we don't filter things out. The ability to stop these thoughts will increase your confidence and ability to gain strength over these negative comments.

(2) *Write negative self-talk thoughts in your journal.* At the end of the day, cross out the negative self-talk and replace with positive self-talk comments.

I recently wrote in my journal for thirty days before my second marathon. During this time, my mind told me I needed more rest before I could run another marathon. I scratched out that thought and replaced it with:

So proud that I ran two marathons in thirty days and I feel great!

I ran my second-fastest marathon of the eight marathons I've run to date.

Write a summary of your thoughts every day before you go to bed so you have these positive affirmations before you sleep. This technique identifies triggers and patterns that bring those positive thoughts to the forefront. This wonderful technique will allow you to move forward with your life and achieve all the success you desire.

(3) **Stop negative thoughts with positive affirmations**. Always tell yourself, "You *can* do this, you *will* do this, and you *must* do this." Get in the habit of saying to yourself, "I am the best, I can do this, I deserve the best, and I will make all my dreams come true!" The amazing Les Brown exclaims at the top of his lungs all the time, "I'm unstoppable!" ...You must remind yourself this all the time, just like Les Brown—you are unstoppable!

The quote at the beginning of this section changed my life. I watched a seminar by Dr. Wayne Dyer and Dr. Chopra on getting beyond the approval of others. Dr. Chopra reminds us that if you can grasp this concept of relinquishing the need to *control*, the need to be *approved*, and the need to *judge*, you are on your way to not only self-talk mastery but also to absolute life bliss! You must try this! Go an entire day without worrying what someone thinks of you.

This is amazing! I'm now free every day!

Why Not Me?

It is not the mountain we conquer but ourselves.

Edmund Hillary

Jim Glick, one of my great friends, mentors, and an amazing trainer and speaker, noticed during the fourth week of treatment that I had changed a bit. The University of Kansas Cancer Center is extremely meticulous with all protocol during treatment and warned everyone to watch for any signs of depression. Even the most motivated person in the world is subject to slip into depression without knowing during intensive chemotherapy and radiation. I drew into negative self-talk and minor depression during my fourth week of treatment.

Jim noticed my attitude had slipped and gave me a call with some great advice.

Instead of hearing the self-talk of *Why me*, he said, change that to *Why not me?* "Who else would you rather have this cancer—your mom, your dad, kids, or loved ones?" Jim asked. "You're fit, have a great attitude, are a motivational speaker, have a military discipline and background. You will use this situation to show others they can overcome adversity and illness."

I never realized I had slipped into any type of depression. I was always sky high, and others also noticed when I dropped a step.

Negative thoughts will always try to enter your mind when the body is weakened. Decide how much power you give your thoughts, and choose the way those thoughts are used. Just like my friend Jim Glick, you need friends watching your behavior and mood for any subtle changes. This is important in everything from daily life to a serious illness. You need that close circle of trust and friends. Being in total control is the biggest self-confidence boost you can get. You have the ability to say good-bye to *Why me*? And hello to my new long-term friend, *Why not me?*

No Pity Parties

Don't live your life to please other people.

Oprah Winfrey

Are you one of those people who expends a tremendous amount of personal energy trying to please others all the time? Amazing transformation happens when you get diagnosed with a serious illness. There is no energy required to find your true friends; they will seek you out.

As Ms. Winfrey stated above about pleasing others, you don't need to please your true friends; they will always be there for you. Save all that energy for other endeavors.

I conducted internal self-talk pity parties when I was initially diagnosed with cancer: *Why me? How can this have happened to me? This is unfair!* Whether I realized it or not, I was having a full-blown pity party with negative self-talk. The problem was that nobody attended my party.

Remember the quote below when you feel like sharing your problems with others:

> *Eighty percent of the people don't want to hear your problems and the other twenty percent are glad it's you and not them.*
>   Lou Holtz

I was alone in my misery. This is when you'll need that extra energy and strength. Focus on you and your task at hand. Use positive visualization and positivity in order to combat negative self-talk. Tell yourself over and over and over again that *you can do this!*

I carried this quote below by Ms. Rosa Parks in my pocket during cancer treatment for the daily inner positive self-talk I needed on some of the very tough days:

> *I have learned over the years that when one's mind is made up, this diminishes fear; knowing what must be done does away with fear.*

What is Your Bulletin Board Material (BBM)?

Things change for the better when we take responsibility for our own thoughts, decisions, and actions.

Eric Thomas

Bulletin Board Material (BBM), also referred to as the locker room wall material, is a metaphor for your reason for striving for success. This is a written reminder or metaphor (like my empty high school diploma case) of why you stay motivated and focused.

What is your Bulletin Board Material? What drives you every day? Why is it you want to go where you want to go? You will find these answers as you focus on what is your *why*. Your BBM will erase the negative internal dialogue, and the positive internal dialogue will drive you through any barrier.

What is your *why* to your BBM? Your kids? Your mother or father? Not graduating high school? Nobody in your family ever attended or graduated from college?

Clearly defining your BBM is a great long-term motivational tool.

Write down your BBM and place in a visible location. You want to see this word, quote, or statement all the time. Keep it in your wallet, purse, and on your office wall...everywhere! Let this BBM remind you why you work relentlessly toward this reminder and goal.

Action

Find a private place and get loud! Think about
that mantra: I will, I can, and I must

You are going to get loud and motivate yourself. Talk to yourself and get yourself fired up. Listen to one of your favorite speakers such as Zig Ziglar, Jack Canfield, Les Brown, or listen to some motivating music. Go for a run and get totally psyched up! Whatever it takes to get you fired up!

Now, turn it all off immediately and go somewhere quiet by yourself. Put yourself in a meditative state. Think about one dream you wanted to achieve. Think about that mantra:

I will, I can, and I must!

Now is the time for you to be your own coach. Do it now! Put those five goals on your BBM. We will link those dreams with goals that will ensure success later in the book.

Daily positive self-message/text

Demaryius Thomas of the Denver Broncos has a unique way of ensuring that he has a positive message every day. Many times, the life in the National Football League can remove him from the memories of his difficult childhood with his mom and grandmother serving sentences in prison. Demaryius begins every day by sending himself a positive text message to remind him to be thankful for what he has. This activity kick-starts his positive self-talk every day.

Send yourself a positive self-message for the next five days. See the amazing transformation that occurs. You will get the positive benefit of self-talk twice every day when you send and receive the positive message. I send this note to myself every day:

> *Greg! Never forget 10 May 2010; be thankful for every breath.*
> *Live every moment the way you did the twenty-four hours after diagnosis.*

Key Points

- Stop negative self-talk in its tracks
- Only listen to positive messages
- Defend your *schloss*
- No pity parties allowed!
- Find your BBM and rely on it daily

OPTIMISM

Chapter Three

Practice Karma Daily

The best way to cheer yourself up is to cheer someone else up.
MARK TWAIN

3

Feng Shui Eyes

Everything has beauty, but not everyone sees it.

CONFUCIUS

Go outside and find a quiet spot.

Close your eyes and slowly breathe in and out through your nose ten times. Breathe long and slow; feel the breath enter and depart your body. Count to five and slowly open your eyes, heart, and mind, and notice all the beautiful abundance around you.

This beautiful place of karma is the bliss known as Feng Shui.

Feng Shui is derived from the Chinese philosophical system of harmonizing everyone with the surrounding environment. I developed my own version of Feng Shui the morning after I was diagnosed with cancer. Feng Shui eyes prepared me to tackle my cancer diagnosis head-on. Your perspective on life changes when you no longer take life for granted.

Before my diagnosis, I had never thought about death. The day after, I walked out the front door of my house and was in another dimension. The whole universe seemed to slow down. Birds sang gleefully, trees were in full bloom, young children played in the paradise of fresh-cut grass, and a monarch butter-fly fluttered by as I walked down my steps on the front porch. The texture of my hands seemed different, as did the clear smell of the fresh paint on the neighbor's house. The Mercedes across the street with the "new purchase" sticker on the window made me think of healthier times in Germany. Golfers across the street strolled toward the seventeenth fairway, and I noticed my Christmas lights were still in the tree on my front lawn—and it was May.

My usually introverted neighbor, standing in his front yard, waved and said, "Hey, how are you doing?" Outside of my family, I did not tell anyone of my diagnosis, but people could clearly see that I was enjoying every second of life.

It seemed I had a flow to life and everything around me.

Suddenly people wanted to interact and just chat with me. Time seemed weightless and inconsequential. My subconscious felt like I was on the movie set of *Pleasantville*.

I lived more in the first hour of the first day after my diagnosis than I had the previous year.

I soon found out the severity of my stage III cancer diagnosis. That did not deepen my spirits; it raised my expectations to maximize all 1,440 minutes of every day and take one hour at a time. My heart and soul were open to all the graciousness of the world. I didn't feel sick; instead, I felt that my body needed a change of daily stagnation. The supply of goodness in the world is endless.

Try to find your Feng Shui eyes daily, and you will see life differently. It will take some focus, but you can do it and watch the change in your entire world.

Pay it Forward Every Day

You can have everything in life you want if you'll just help enough other people to get what they want!

Zig Ziglar

This is one of my favorite activities in the world and I love it!

Pay it forward is an expression for describing being the beneficiary of a good deed and repaying it to others instead of to the original benefactor. Paying it forward is magical and works for everyone. This is the epic result of the law of attraction, we seem to always think and attract what we think. Connect to negative, and negative people and negative situations will find you every day of the week.

Random acts of kindness will not only pay increased dividends for the receiver of the act, but also for the sender and others around. This act of gratitude just works its way around the entire compass of supportive people. At your next opportunity, try leaving an appreciation note, paying for a coffee, or covering a meal at a restaurant before the bill arrives. Notice how amazing you feel afterward...and the rest will take care of itself.

Create Cancer Center Karma (Karma Squared)

Always give without remembering and always receive without forgetting.

Brian Tracy

My Feng Shui eyes and soul were put into a state of uncertainty and fear during my first official visit to the University of Kansas

(KU) Cancer Center. Despite the KU Cancer Center being an amazing state-of-the-art medical center with elite technology, it is still a cancer center and can be an intimidating place. The entire reception room—patient entrance, employees, administrators, patients, family, and friends—everyone was very subdued.

The tension was thick as I made my way into the waiting room and toward the reception desk. The receptionist handed me an initial stack of forms to fill out. It felt like I was just another patient walking the "Green Mile" of cancer. I waited for a seat to become available as patients filled out stacks of forms on clipboards and loved ones hung on with a sense of nervousness for the unknown of what the future holds.

I've filled out hundreds, if not thousands, of medical forms during my twenty-plus year military career. My breath caught in my throat when I came to the question, *Have you ever had a serious illness?*

Check. Yes…cancer.

I looked around the room and thought, *Is this real?* It actually hit me as if I was in denial until this moment. *Am I really being seen for cancer?*

My initial appointment included more sticking, poking, and prodding than I had received in the past twenty years. The grand finale of the first day was the numerous needle biopsies through my neck into the tumor to confirm the staging of the cancer. I departed after a tense and stressful first day with follow-up instructions to meet my entire medical team the following day.

I stepped outside the cancer center under a breezeway, and I noticed a thin elderly man with a port in his arm for IV fluids. The gentleman looked distracted and I struck up a conversation about his cap he wore from the Negro Leagues Baseball Museum in Kansas City. He immediately lit up, and we talked about Satchel

Paige, Ernie Banks, Buck O'Neil, and the Kansas City Monarchs for thirty minutes.

He had just finished radiation therapy and was waiting for a taxi that was apparently not in a hurry to get him. I asked if he had any family to pick him up. He replied, "They are all too busy right now." The taxi showed up and the man struggled as I helped him into the cab. I paid it forward and gave the man a military coin I had recently received in Korea and paid for the taxi.

I never asked him if he was a military veteran; I assumed he was by his large smile as he looked at the Second Infantry Division logo on the coin, as if to reminisce about his younger days. I watched as he drove away and he waved good-bye with a smile. I had a filled heart. Unfortunately, I never saw the gentleman again.

This is the story of the cancer center. I met amazing people battling insurmountable odds every day. They would be here one day and then suddenly disappear.

As the cab pulled away and drove off, I decided I was going to embark on a journey that is contrary from the karma I felt when I walked into the cancer center. I was walking around with a new fresh set of Feng Shui eyes; I was seeing things as I never did before. I told myself I was going to reverse the karma at the cancer center (karma squared), and my goal every day was to come to treatment and serve, satisfy, and put the needs and concerns of everyone else before my needs.

I will serve my medical staff, doctors, nurses, healthcare staff, and even the other patients above me and pay it forward. I will give to others, and the karma will be returned to others. The universe will just make this happen. I will thank everyone for all they do. My passion and only goal is to change the karma of the cancer center.

I carried around a set of three quotations the entire eight weeks of radiation and chemotherapy:

Who is the happiest of men? He who values the merits of others, and in their pleasure takes joy, even as though it were his own.

Johann Wolfgang von Goethe

Seize the moments of happiness, love and be loved! That is the only reality in the world; all else is folly.

Leo Tolstoy

Happiness is not something ready-made. It comes from our own actions.

Mahatma Gandhi

An amazing transformation began on the fifth day of radiation and chemotherapy. The more I focused on everyone else, the better I felt. Everything became easier. I found stillness in radiation, discovered yoga, practiced daily meditation, and established complete focus on others. I didn't focus on the fight against cancer anymore; I focused on being cancer-free. The universe was in harmony with my flow!

I gained strength with every thank you card I presented, every milkshake handed to the receptionists, and every greeting and hug for each of the doctors and nurses. I felt the entire staff anticipating my arrival at treatment every day. Instead of chaos, everything flowed in harmony.

Wow! I was greeted every day with hugs, laughter, stories, and smiles from everyone from the custodial staff, support staff, snack bar, medical technicians, patients, doctors, and department directors. I felt my body regaining the momentum and regaining control. The karma was flowing my way in abundance as I gave others the power of Feng Shui and they, in turn, gave it back to everyone else in the hospital.

I felt the cancer not just retreating from my body, but also running away!

My radiation physician, Dr. Pravesh Kumar, with twenty-five years experience and regarded by his peers as one of the best radiologists in the country, told me in week four, "I've never seen a tumor of that size disappear so fast—it's remarkable."

I was healing so quickly because I had become a healing force for the doctors and nurses in the cancer center. The field of oncology is extremely rewarding and likewise can be emotionally devastating to the doctors, nurses, and entire staff. Medical staffs are charged with dealing with extremely long hours, insurmountable stress, and lines and lines of patients battling a severe illness day after day.

I've spent sixteen years in the medical field as an administrator, and I've seen healthcare professionals—and especially those in the field of cancer—stricken with depression, fatigue, PTSD, and suicide. My actions are directed at healing my doctors with attitude, and that will allow my doctors and nurses to give a hundred percent in returning the karma to everyone in the cancer center, including healthcare providers themselves—wow! Did it ever work! Amazing!

Dr. Kumar brought the medical students in throughout the last four weeks of treatment to show them the original x-rays of the tumor. He showed the students how big the tumor was at the present time, and they were all shocked at the rapid decrease in the size of the tumor.

BLUF: CANCER HATES HAPPINESS!

Today, the seven-centimeter tumor is completely gone and the scar is transparent. I attribute focusing my gratitude on others as the key to reversing the karma in the cancer center and also my own health. The tremendous overflow of karma coming back to me is an absolute contributing factor in my successful treatment and becoming cancer-free.

Every day, I could feel myself acquiring more and more strength as the cancer rushed out of my body. Simultaneously, I felt the karma of everybody within the cancer center. How many patients look forward to treatment? I anxiously anticipated treatment every day and having the chance to bring fun and laughter to my doctors and nurses.

Action

Daily alone time

> *My ability to embrace stillness and meditation was the momentum swing in my health transformation. I breathed in and out with the musical sounds of the Pacific Ocean. I breathed in life, energy, and the universe and as I breathed out, I felt every red and white blood cell washing the cancer cells out to sea with the waves.*

The Dali Lama reminds us silence is best.

Go find a quiet place and reflect on all that you have to be thankful for. Silence your mind. Simple thoughts placed in your heart will put energy in motion and immediately fill your soul. Write down in your journal how this practice makes you feel. Silence is amazing!

Attack those negative thoughts for the first three minutes of every day

You will not give any negative thoughts the chance of interfering with your day of karma. The first three minutes set the tone for the rest of the day.

Recall your self-talk journal notes as you notated any negative self-talk and replaced it with positive thoughts in your journal. Closely follow the next three steps:

1. Start the day off by reading all the positive thoughts from the day before.

2. Now re-read each one and add five things you are thankful for today.

3. Repeat this process daily. Watch the start of the day begin with complete optimism, and you will be prepared to seize the day.

Key Points

- Locate your Feng Shui eyes daily
- Pay it forward every opportunity you have
- Create good karma...and it will come back to you!
- Seek to heal and improve others with your attitudes
- Center yourself with alone time every day

OPTIMISM

Chapter Four

Integrate Thanks into Your Daily Life

Every time we remember to say "thank you,"
we experience nothing less than Heaven on Earth.

SARAH BAN BREATHNACH

4

Just Be Thankful

I can no other answer make but thanks, and thanks.

SHAKESPEARE

Being thankful must became part of your daily routine.

The Three Points of Contact and achieving your dreams are tied directly to giving thanks. I can attribute overcoming adversity and achieving success to integrating thanks into everything I do. The secret of being thankful is getting into the routine of always looking for someone to thank.

Giving thanks will always make you feel better.

My mother taught me when I was young: Always, always say thank you and be thankful. I grew up around drugs, alcohol, crime, and every other opportunity to get into trouble. The chance to get into mischief was always available since my mom worked multiple jobs and normally worked nights. I never did drugs or drank alcohol, and I stayed completely clear of trouble, as I knew it would crush my mother. My mom has always been my Bulletin Board Material (BBM)—even before I realized it. Saying thanks, being grateful and optimistic made me feel good, even when we didn't have anything.

My mother did all she could to make sure we at least had the minimum essentials in life as our family struggled. We went months eating macaroni and cheese, and many times we barely had enough food to put on the table. My mom would get me up at 4:30 AM so I could get the old bread off the baker's rack when the market opened. I would always tell my mom thanks for what we had, and it made everything better.

> *All that I am and all I hope to be, I owe to my mother.*
>   Abraham Lincoln

Like many of you, our mothers are the major influences in our lives. My mother laid the foundation for my optimistic behavior throughout my entire life. I was—and still am—thankful for the jobs and the shelter my mother was able to provide.

The most telling part of my research came from Dr. Martin Seligman, professor of psychology at the University of Pennsylvania and author of *Learned Optimism: How to Change Your Mind and Your Life.* "There is a markedly high correlation between your level of optimism and your mother's, but not your father's," Seligman stated. Although no one knows why this is, one hypothesis is that mothers still tend to be primary caretakers and therefore have a greater influence on their offspring. Another theory is that women have evolved to be more cerebral and expressive, so they're more likely to communicate their outlook, positive or negative.

I find this to be a striking fact in my experience with my mother. No matter how bad things got for us when we were young, my mother was always optimistic…and that sense of learned optimism has stayed with me forever.

The Handwritten Thank You Note

You may have a Porsche, a mansion, a vacation home, and all the money in the world. However, I have the handwritten thank you note, the greatest heartfelt equalizer of all time.

Handwritten thank you notes have been a part of my life since I was a child. I'm sure my mother wrote a thank you note to the doctor who delivered me when I was born. It was only a matter of time, and I was soon caught up in the knack of writing thank you notes. I've absorbed the amazing feeling I get from leaving a thank you note for someone or putting the note in the mail.

I first used thank you notes when I was a thirteen-year-old caddie in Sacramento. I would pedal my bicycle to the other side of town and be the first one into the golf caddie shack. If I was lucky, I would get a loop, which is what caddies call carrying clubs for eighteen holes. If I could get a loop in the morning and one in the afternoon, that was a good payday for me. I soon began to realize that as a thirteen-year-old, I needed to differentiate myself from the older teens and adults competing for weekend caddie jobs. I began to incorporate my mom's number one rule of handwritten thank you notes after every round I caddied. For the next four years, I worked every weekend morning and afternoon loop, and I was always requested first before the other caddies.

The thank you note was my first marketing and networking tool.

Happiness does not magically appear because you have a big house, a high-paying job, a fancy car, a vacation home, and lots of money. Many of the unhappiest, most unpleasant, bitter, chronically pessimistic, and ungrateful people I've ever met in my travels around the world had all of these things…the problem is they were tied up in only thinking of these materialistic values and never stopped to be thankful. I've handed out thousands of thank you notes since my caddying days in Sacramento. Think about this:

I never received a thank you note from a miserable, pessimistic, and unhappy person.

My mother did not have much money, education, or any fancy toys for herself or to give us, yet she is the happiest person I've ever known. My mother's secret to being happy was giving thanks. The gift that my mom received was bigger than any monetary value.

My mother's happiness is from the joy she received by giving thanks.

Thank You Notes Are Good for Your Health

Be thankful for what you have; you'll end up having more. If you concentrate on what you don't have, you will never, ever have enough.

Oprah Winfrey

Research suggests that individuals who are grateful in their daily lives report fewer stress-related health problems such as headaches, stomach issues, chest pain, muscle aches, appetite problems, and a list of other medical problems, says Sheila Raja, PhD, a clinical psychologist at the University of Illinois at Chicago. Thankful people are also often more content because they don't spend a lot of time comparing themselves with others.

The combination of stillness, focus, and sending thank you notes to my medical staff at the cancer center made going to each appointment an *opportunity* and not treatment, radiation, chemotherapy, or cancer as a *problem*. You will become so enthralled in giving thanks, you will forget about the situation at hand.

I have an activity that I do with my students at the end of each public speaking class. Upon the completion of the final speeches, each student will get a thank you card from me with their final grade.

Before they leave the class for the final time, I ask the students to think about their educational experience and one person they want to thank for the opportunity of attending this wonderful college or university. The recipient of the thank you note can be local or halfway around the world. The students address the envelope and I have stamps at the front table. I do not mail the note for the students. I want them to take in the wonderful feeling when they drop the thank you note off at the post office. I asked my students to contact me after they send the thank you note to tell me how they feel.

After the semester is over, I usually receive a response from the majority of my students telling me how wonderful it felt over the following twenty-four hours after sending the thank you note. Look at the attitude change that ensued by sending just one thank you card!

I offer every student with a passing grade the opportunity to contact me for a letter of recommendation. I've written more than 700 letters of recommendations—for graduate school, employment, or other opportunities—for my prior students around the world. As with the thank you notes, the gratitude of offering a letter of recommendation for a student looking to climb the ladder either in education or toward professional growth gives me absolute satisfaction.

Go to a local store today and buy a box of thank you cards, or get some colorful 3x5 cards and envelopes. Get into the habit of sending daily thank you cards/notes and experience the transformation that happens in your life.

The Activity Importance of Thank You Notes in the Digital Age

The Internet is so big, so powerful and pointless, that for some people it is a complete substitute for life.

Andrew Brown

Saying thank you through digital media such as Facebook, Twitter, e-mail, LinkedIn, and every other form of electronic media has become commonplace. This method is not only impersonal, but you also don't receive the same extraordinary feeling you will get from the handwritten thank you note. The handwritten note will change your health, disposition, and distinguish you from everyone else.

Send a thank you note today. Give it a try now and see the amazing feeling you get from such a simple gesture.

The Benefits of Sending Thank You Notes

Let us rise up and be thankful, for if we didn't learn a lot today, at least we learned a little, and if we didn't learn a little,

at least we didn't get sick, and if we got sick, at least we didn't
die; so, let us all be thankful.

Buddha

The benefits of sending handwritten thank you notes are end-less. You are doing far more than distinguishing yourself from any-one else in the business world or your competition. That person may have met twenty other people today, yet you will be remembered for leaving the thank you note. Business is about making contacts, and the thank you note is the best way to make an impression...and will also make you feel amazing. Advantages of the thank you note:

- Feel great about yourself
- Relieve stress, which makes you a healthier and happier person
- Relieve the recipients' stress, thus making them and yourself healthier
- Create a positive impact to those receiving your thanks, making you more memorable and making you stand out from others
- Put a smile on someone's face

Try sending out thank you notes at every opportunity you get: Thank someone who hosts you at his or her house for dinner, someone who sends you a gift, someone who provides a service... the list goes on and on. Starting with the first thank you note you send, you'll notice a difference in the mental, emotional, and spiritual quality of your life.

How to Write the Perfect Thank You Note

If the only prayer you ever say your entire life is thank you, then that's enough.

Meister Eckhart

My first thank you note was to a golfer I caddied for when I was thirteen years old. Since then, I have written thousands of these wonderful notes. I have my own personal techniques I've learned over the years, and you will develop your own style There's actually a recommended tactic to ensure you write the perfect thank you note. Diane Gottsman, a national etiquette expert and the owner of the Protocol School of Texas, recommends:

- A handwritten note is always special.
- Use a dark-colored ink, preferably black, when sending a professional thank you note.
- Address the card carefully, making sure the name of the person is spelled accurately.
- Mention something specific about the gift, if applicable, and how you plan to use or enjoy it in the future.
- Don't mention a denomination of money; rather, say your "generous" gift.
- Purchase nice, seasonal stamps or invest in forever stamps.
- Create a thank you note cache that is easily accessible when you are ready to sit down and write a thank you note. Include nice card stock, stamps, and a variety of writing pens and note cards.

Recommended Read: *A Simple Act of Gratitude*

Thanks, sir; all the rest is mute.

Shakespeare

John Kralik, author of the New York Times bestseller *A Simple Act of Gratitude*, penned an entire book on how learning to say "thank you" changed his life! Mr. Kralik's autobiography follows his story of sending a thank you note every day for one year. As a lawyer with a failing law firm and struggling through a painful divorce, Kralik grew distant from his children and his life dreams were slipping beyond his reach. Mr. Kralik decided a way of being grateful was to set a goal of writing 365 notes in the coming year. After sending the first couple notes, significant surprising benefits began to come his way—financial gain, friendship, weight loss, and inner peace. One by one, each thank you note began to turn his entire life around.

Action

Thanks one day at a time for one month

Write a list of all the people to whom you would like to write a thank you note. Think of everybody from friends, family, colleagues, and people you meet on a daily basis. Using the simple rules that we talked about earlier in writing a thank you note, write one note every day for thirty days.

I guarantee at the end of thirty days you will see the magnificent feeling you get from writing these notes of thanks and gratitude. Send me a note and tell me how you feel after this action. Did you continue on past thirty days?

Write a thank you letter to yourself

Write a thank you letter to yourself to show thanks for a great accomplishment you will achieve in the future. Write the note dated one year from today. Thank yourself for agreeing to accomplish a set dream, goal, or objective. Writing this letter will hold yourself accountable to complete a mission that you have defined. Studies show that you are more apt to complete a task you have held yourself responsible for. You may write the "thank yourself note" for later today, tomorrow, next week or next month…. Just thank yourself!

It works and I recently used it myself. I wrote this thank you to myself on November 30, 2013:

Congratulations, Greg, for finishing three marathons in the past year for a total of seven! Where will you run to celebrate five years cancer-free in July 2015?

On July 30, 2014, I wrote myself a note to congratulate myself on being five years cancer-free on July 30, 2015. What a joy it will be to open that letter!

Key Points

- Be thankful for everything, no matter how small
- Send thank you notes at every opportunity
- Sending thank you notes has been proven to increase health and well being
- Handwritten thank you notes are rare and perceived as special

VISUALIZATION

VISUALIZATION

VISUALIZATION

Chapter Five

Turn It All Off and Empty Your Cup

"Namaste"

The ability to be in the present moment
is a major component of mental wellness.

ABRAHAM MASLOW

5

Empty Your Cup

*Learning how to be still, to really be still and let life
happen - that stillness becomes a radiance.*

MORGAN FREEMAN

A university professor went to visit a famous Zen master. While
the master quietly served tea, the professor talked about Zen, holding himself forth as an expert on the topic. The master poured
the visitor's cup to the brim, and then kept pouring. The professor watched the overflowing cup until he could no longer restrain
himself. "It's overfilled! No more will go in!" the professor blurted.
"You are like this cup," the master replied. "How can I show you
Zen unless you first empty your cup?"

This chapter is about completely emptying your cup, and finding your stillness through yoga, locating that happy place, finding
peace, bliss, and quieting the mind—enjoy.

Cancer Hates Stillness

In the midst of movement and chaos, keep stillness inside of you.

Deepak Chopra

I used stillness to run cancer from my body.

There's a time in any battle when the victor begins to get that competitive edge. You feel the emotion or tide turning. Watch any sporting event, you'll hear the announcer say, "The team has gained the momentum."

The other team might be more talented, bigger, and stronger... but you can feel the other team gaining the momentum and the game immediately starts turning the other way. The ability to quiet yourself, get into the flow, and solely focus on being clear of negativity is the key to stillness—or in my case, letting the cancer retreat from my body!

Through silencing my body, I felt my body being cleansed cell by cell—and that is the genius of this chapter. This is when I stopped battling cancer and focused on being cancer-free. Instead of being filled with pain, lack of sleep, stress, anxiety, and intermediate depression, I was able to find my true stillness and change the tide and take control.

Until my mind was set free and my cup empty, I was not able to settle in on my vision and truly have the opportunity to take action against cancer.

I've accomplished so much since my diagnosis because of finding that stillness. I've started my life all over again by moving to Europe, starting a new business, writing a book, running multiple marathons, performing motivational coaching and speaking around the world, teaching more college classes, and loving life! All this in the four years since my cancer diagnosis!

The tests show that stress most likely caused my cancer. Achieving stillness allowed my body to regain control and move toward a cancer-free future.

Coach V Had it Right!

Yoga doesn't take time, it gives time.

Ganga White

Jimmy Valvano was an amazing college basketball coach who passed away of cancer. Jimmy Valvano, who was also known simply by most in the sports world as "Coach V," founded the V Foundation of Cancer Research prior to his passing. It wasn't until my cancer diagnosis that I finally discovered what Coach V actually meant in his description of the three things we all should do every day.

I remember watching the famous Jimmy V speech, "Don't Ever Give Up Cancer" at the 1993 ESPY Awards at Madison Square Garden. I was a captain in the US Army, stationed at Fort Carson, Colorado, and a couple months away from finishing graduate school at the University of Northern Colorado. I had just returned from a tour in Germany serving in Operation Desert Shield and Desert Storm. We also had a one-year-old son, Erik, and later in the year we would have our first daughter, Nicole.

My memory of the presentation was extremely touching; I remember hurriedly writing down his three key points from the presentation on a napkin and telling myself, "I will figure out a way to do all three of those every day as Jimmy V suggested." Coach captivated the nation with this presentation. Coach made his famous quote below, which lives with me every day.

There are three things we all should do every day of our lives.

1. *You should laugh every day.*
2. *Think. You should spend some time in thought.*
3. *You should have your emotions moved to tears, could be happiness or joy.*

Coach V proclaimed, "But think about it. If you laugh, you think, and you cry, that's a full day. That's a heck of a day. You do that seven days a week, you're going to have something special."

Coach V stated that if we do these things every day, it would be a perfect day. But in every day, it's important to remember the following quote from Ralph Waldo Emerson:

Nothing was ever achieved without enthusiasm.

I've watched this speech a hundred times to get motivated for various situations long before I was diagnosed with cancer. Yet, I couldn't bring myself to watch the video after I was diagnosed with cancer.

I watched the clip again with my college students after my diagnosis, and I finally realized what Coach Valvano was taking about.

Cancer taught me to cherish the opportunity to laugh, think, and bring my emotions to tears every day. Don't wait for cancer or some other illness or tragedy; do this every day. Share your thoughts with me—I can't wait to hear your experiences.

Find Your Yoga and Stillness

Yoga accepts, yoga gives.

Terri Guillemets

I remember the day like it was yesterday, although it was almost five years ago: I had just completed my second week of radiation and chemotherapy at the University of Kansas Cancer Center. The massive dose of radiation I was receiving made me feel like I just left a microwave—my entire upper body felt scorched and burned from my shoulders to the top of my head. I was lightheaded, had begun losing my taste buds, and was starting to lose weight.

I couldn't get myself to become still and relax. I had hundreds of negative thoughts in my head that consumed my very being. I could drop the negative thoughts for just a brief moment and then they returned!

Thoughts of cancer, my death, my wake, funeral, my children, family, parents, friends, death again, more cancer and...*why me?* Can I get everything done before I die? Do I have time for a bucket list? Who am I kidding—my bucket list is now spending what time I have left with my children and the people I love! These thoughts were with me day and night, without a moment's break. I could not focus and concentrate on my cancer treatment with all these negative self-talk thoughts!

I completed my tenth day of radiation, and I wanted to go for a walk and be alone after treatment. I put on my big golf hat, which became routine to shade myself from the intense heat of the June sun. My treatment was always mid-day and my entire body became extremely sensitive to the heat. I walked out of the medical center, down Rainbow Boulevard, and I felt my stomach tube become a bit loose; it was leaking, as I felt the warm fluid on my stomach. I tightened the fastener and took a right on 39th Street, heading straight toward Chipotle Mexican Grill. I had no appetite, so I paid for the meal of the next person in line—it always feels good to pay it forward. The building was air-conditioned, everyone was friendly, and nobody treated me like I had a severe illness; I was just a customer. I sat in the dining area just drinking ice water, giving myself the best motivational speech I possibly could. I was pulling out all the quotes and cards from all the world's best motivational speakers. My mind was racing—six more weeks of chemotherapy and radiation. *I must find a way to get control back.*

After an hour, I left Chipotle and wanted to walk away from the cancer center, as I was trying to self-talk motivate myself and move the cancer thoughts out of my mind.

I noticed the words on the building up ahead proudly proclaimed *Bikram Yoga*. I've done yoga off and on during my military career to calm stress, and it has worked extremely well. I've even tried "Bikram" hot yoga a couple times in my travels and it whooped me good. I remember doing Bikram in Boise, Idaho, and all I could do was drink water for the next twenty-four hours as I recovered. Surely doing ninety minutes of yoga at a hundred-plus degrees and twenty-six positions is not the best idea for a cancer patient? I still had six weeks left of treatment, a PEG stomach tube inserted through my abdominal wall, and I would soon be feeding myself entirely through my stomach when I completely lost my taste buds and my throat closed shut.

The universe pulled me to the door of this Bikram yoga studio. The director of the studio, Angela Moulin, asked me to come in, and we began to talk about my rather unique situation. I walked into the studio with a thousand thoughts in my head, convincing myself that I needed to find a way to maintain a meditative state. I was able to meditate during radiation as I meditated into my "German" happy place.

I was able to get into a flow during both radiation and chemotherapy treatment. However, once I left the cancer center, I could not clear these thoughts. I always felt cancer was watching my every move. This feeling ended once I entered the yoga studio.

Cancer was stopped at the door at Angela's Kansas City Bikram yoga studio. My thoughts of cancer were not allowed in the studio and cancer did not dare enter. My mind became completely clear and the catastrophic cancer thoughts stopped.

Wow! I mean, everything stopped at the door. Seemed the force of dozens of meditating and peaceful yoga practitioners was too much for those thoughts.

I was a hundred percent cancer-thought-free from the time I walked into the studio for the entire ninety-minute practice. This was the beginning of the end of me thinking about cancer! Within a couple weeks of yoga practice, I was cancer-thought-free twenty-four hours a day! Absolutely no more negative cancer thoughts, nightmares, and I found complete stillness without a thought about cancer.

Yoga, the fellow students, staff, and the much-needed meditation helped me control those thoughts, and I only thought about being cancer-free, and I realized: At this point…

I already am cancer-free!

I travel and speak all over the world, and to this day, have practiced at studios in more than ten countries. Whether Hatha, Vinyasa, Bikram, Kundalini, or power, the atmosphere in these yoga studios are all the same. Amazing and incredibly supportive people in every studio! Negativity, anger, depression, and all negative thoughts, including cancer, are never allowed in the studio.

As I reviewed my journal notes of this entire experience, practicing yoga is the turning point when cancer completely lost the edge and I regained the momentum! Yoga helped me feel like I was in complete charge again. My Namaste with the yoga community allowed me to not look at cancer as a fight or battle. I focused on the happy end state when this treatment is complete. My mind is now free.

Thanks to yoga, I live every day in absolute bliss.
Namaste!

Find Your Happy Place

Yoga is the practice of quieting the mind.

Patanjali

The magnificent little story of the guru at the start of this chapter was shared with me by Galen Pearl, author of *Ten Steps to Find Your Happy Place*. It's true—we cannot get to a point of a true happy place until we completely empty the cup.

My amazing medical team had me on a very tight and precise radiation therapy regimen that included a massive amount of radiation. Radiation took place five days a week for eight weeks. I was fitted with a mesh plastic radiotherapy mask, the nurses placed the mask on my face and screwed the mask and my head to the table—so I couldn't move or slip during the radiation treatment. The staff made me as comfortable as possible with soft music and professional customer service beyond reproach. When I was placed inside the small entrance of the Varian Linear Accelerator for my radiation treatment, the claustrophobia still got to me, and I had to be sedated so I could relax during the radiation therapy.

I needed to find a way to relax during radiation. I felt the radiation was not being effective while I was being sedated. The very experienced radiology tech mentioned finding a "happy place" to relax while I was in radiation. She mentioned thinking of a place that I was in absolute bliss and relaxation.

I was the happiest in my life as a brand-new US Army second lieutenant stationed in Stuttgart, Germany. Germany was completely different from anything I'd ever experienced in my life. The people were so friendly, everything was immaculately clean. I enjoyed the culture, the food, and especially the soccer matches…I just loved it all. I immediately told the radiation tech I wanted to do the radiation without the drugs.

I closed my eyes, and I put myself in Germany as the mask was tightened across my face and onto my head, each bolt being fastened to the flat x-ray table. The plastic squares dug into my forehead and neck. My mind shifted to Germany and its little towns, the food, smooth public transportation, the friendly people, the beautiful summers, and fantastic winters. I visually put myself at a German Bundesliga soccer match. I'm there; I can hear the fans, smell the food, hear the cheers, and see the teams. I found my happy place and was able to completely relax.

By the time I was done with treatment, I promised myself that I would go live and work in Germany within the next year. *I'm not sure how this is going to happen. I will let my newfound happy place, the power of the universe, stillness, calm, and meditation show me the way.*

Action

The 30-day Challenge – Give Yoga a Chance

Challenge yourself to complete any type of yoga for thirty consecutive days. That's it—pure and simple.

Why do it? Experience the amazing physical, mental, and physiological benefits of a daily practice. Enjoy a wide range of benefits, including stress reduction, weight loss, and an improved overall sense of well-being! I just completed thirty days—it's transformational.

Go Find Your Happy Place – Really…Find Your Happy Place

Where is the happiest place you've ever been? Take a really good look at your life. When were you most happy? With family, on vacation, at the ocean, the mountains, a river, with your parents, your spouse? Turn out the lights, get a small blanket, and lie on the floor on your back. Put your hands out, palms face up, and slowly feel yourself breathe in through the nose and out through the mouth. Go into this happy place and make it as descriptive and vivid as you can.

I visualized leaving the cancer center, driving to the airport, getting on the flight to Germany, and arriving in Germany. I could smell the bread cooking in the bakery. I would buy a German *bretzel*, pay for my train ticket, ride the train to the soccer stadium, buy my match ticket, and sit and watch the soccer match. After the match, I saw my wife and my son Erik when he was little. I placed myself back in the exact same house in Miedelsbach just outside

Stuttgart. This is the happiest moment of my life. Once I embraced this happy place and my stillness, I began to take control of my treatment and focus on being cancer-free. Twenty minutes should be enough time for you to find your complete stillness.

Key Points

- Master the art of Zen for increased well-being and stress relief
- Become still and relaxed—try yoga and meditation
- Find your happy place daily
- Center yourself daily

VISUALIZATION

Chapter Six

Be in the Top Three Percent Now!

Give me a stock clerk with a goal, I'll give you a man that can make history.

Give me a man with no goals and I will give you a stock clerk.

J.C. PENNEY

6

Get Serious about Goal Setting

Setting goals is the first step in turning the invisible into the visible.

TONY ROBBINS

It is time today, right now, to get serious about goal setting. When I lay in bed after being diagnosed with cancer and had a few minutes to myself, my first thought was about the things that I said I was going to do…that I didn't do.

Any time I did not achieve a goal, it was clearly because I was not being specific and I was putting my goals is general terms. I listened to Zig Ziglar a thousand times, and I would slip into one of his favorite quotes: "Don't become a wandering generality, become a meaningful specific." There is an entire world full of people who say they are going to lose weight, they are going to write a book, they are going to achieve a particular task. It wasn't until I was in the hospital bed looking at the ceiling that I realized there were a couple things I never accomplished. I'd always wanted to write a book. I love motivating people and getting them fired up about life. But I had become one of those "I'm going to do this someday" people. I was waiting for the perfect opportunity. But how long would I wait?

I'd always wanted to run a marathon. The 26.2 miles had hung over my head for years and years. I sat in that hospital bed looking at the ceiling. I reached over and grabbed a pen off the table, grabbed a piece of paper, and wrote my first goal: Complete a marathon!

Cancer and Goal Setting

I'm cancer-free today! Cancer cannot keep up with my goals, enthusiasm, focus, passion, and determination. I will run you out of my body by not thinking about you, I will focus on what it will be like when you are gone.

It wasn't until I was diagnosed with cancer that I really got serious about my goals. I've accomplished more goals in the last four and a half years than I did in the previous twenty years. I've completed every goal that I set out to achieve since May 2010:

- Cancer-free by January 2011 (Goal set May 2010)
- Living in Germany by December 2011 (Goal set June 2010)
- Run my first half-marathon by December 2011 (Goal set May 2010)
- Run my first full marathon by June 2011 (Goal set May 2010)
- Run my fifth marathon by December 2014 (Goal set October 2011)
- Write my first book by January 2015 (Goal set August 2012)
- Start my speaking business by January 2015 (Goal set August 2012)
- Lose forty-five pounds by December 2013 (Goal set December 2012)

You Are About to Be in the Top Three Percent

Raise the ceiling and be in the top one percent. Set your goals high, and don't stop till you get there.

Bo Jackson

Statistics have shown that only three percent of the population has well-defined, clear written goals. The three percent with written goals will earn as much as *ten times more* than the ninety-seven percent without written goals.

One of the number-one attributes of extremely successful people is that they think about goals all the time.

One of the greatest lessons I learned as an aide de camp working under senior military officers, including General Colin Powell and General Norman Schwarzkopf, was they always had something to write on at all times. They were always writing in their journals and setting and reassessing their goals. This is why I'm always mentioning the importance of constantly writing in your journal. I've used that lesson my entire life to gain an edge. This way, you can always write down your goals, ideas, thoughts, dreams, and lessons learned. Make sure you write down suggestions, comments, and words of advice you receive.

Successful people assess and discuss their goals all the time!

I've been blessed to spend a majority of my life serving in the United States Armed Forces. I work every day with so many amazing, sharp, intelligent, proactive, energetic people, from enlisted, noncommissioned and commissioned officers, civilians, and flag officers. I speak a lot about studying motivational speakers and goal setting. Executing goals in some of the toughest environments in the world is a completely different story.

I've created a combination of these key points in my life's work, my observations from successful people, working with mentors, and my personal goal-setting experiences.

The following is my six-step process of setting goals. I suggest you write the steps down directly into your journal. Every time you write a goal, write it down with the same process. Now let's start setting goals!

Step 1: Your Goal or Dream
1.   *Write down your goal or your dream.*
It's unfortunate our culture is losing the ability to dream. Do some thinking and let your imagination run wild. Fill up an entire piece of paper with your dreams. You instill hope in your future when you dream, and with hope comes possibility and then the biggest of all attitude behaviors— optimism and enthusiasm.

Write your goal in the future tense. *I will finish college by this date* or *I will earn this much money by this date.* These are positive and effective methods of setting your goals. You are now moving forward. Always start your goals with "I," and put personal responsibility and assignment to yourself for this goal.

2.   ***Now, raise your goal one level.*** This is your new end state and will immediately move you from the top three percent to the top one percent. Whatever your goal or dream is, raise it one full level.

I get ten to fifteen students every semester who are majoring in nursing. I ask these students to write their goals one level up—for example, one level up would be to be a nurse practitioner and they can even try two levels up and that would be to be a doctor. The worst thing that can happen by trying to raise your ceiling is that you end up right back where the ceiling was anyway, so what do you have to lose? Go raise that ceiling!

Step 2: Visualize

Establish a clear visual picture of your goal. Use the four steps below from law of belief section in the text to get into your deep thought visualization. Turn to pages 109 & 110 for the complete definitions of the four ways below to ensure you maintain a clear and positive visualization of your goal.

1. *Frequency: Visualize your goal as often as possible.*
2. *Duration: Hold you visualization as long as you can.*
3. *Clarity: Make your goal crystal clear.*
4. *Intensity: Maintain your intensity with a calm nerve.*

You must see it to achieve it! Silence your mind, and get into deep thought about your end state.

Step 3: Brainstorm, Make a List, and Network Now

1. ***Brainstorm*** a list of all the items you need to achieve this goal. Find a quiet place, get a blank piece of paper, and leave yourself alone for ten to fifteen minutes. For the first five minutes, write down everything you can think of that is related to this goal. Don't stop, just keep writing until the end of five minutes. Don't try to think how you use each one of these, just write and write.
2. ***Make a list.*** The next step is to organize what you have brain-stormed into a single list. Now you can highlight those key areas and assign them to each one of your milestones on your

calendar when you plan backward. Save all your brainstorming topics in your journal. Many times, items that you have excluded after your brainstorming you will be able to use later.

3. ***Network now!*** Contact all your family, friends, organizations, mentors. This is where the importance of networking comes into your life. *Sometimes it's not what you know, but who you know.* This is a critical step in achieving your goal because many people think they must do it all on their own. Nobody does it alone. Anybody who has achieved a significant dream or goal has called upon a friend, colleague, mentor, or has just reached out on a social network to contact somebody for advice on achieving his or her goal. This is the beautiful thing about all the social networking you have at your disposal. Your list should be endless.

Step 4: Set the Suspense, Backward Plan, and Your BBM

1. ***Set the suspense.*** Get a calendar and select that date. You now have a "mark on the wall." Let's do it!

2. ***Backward plan:*** Fill in your calendar from present day to the suspense of your goal or suspense date back to the start date. This backward plan technique is extremely effective and will tighten up your time management and assist greatly in placing your milestones on track. Fill in by hour, day, week, and month—be as detailed and specific as you can. My plan for running a marathon will include specific times each day that I will sleep, run, eat, drink water, cross train, have a massage, visualize, stretch, do yoga, and have free time. These items are specific and written from the start of my training all the way to when I cross the finish line. Everything hour by hour, day by day, week by week, and month by month is all written out.

3. ***BBM:*** Write down your BBM and place in a visible location. You want to see this word, quote, or statement all the time. Keep it in your wallet or purse and on your office wall...everywhere! Let this BBM remind you why you work relentlessly toward this reminder and goal.

Step 5: Take Action Now!

1. ***Take action now!*** Many people never achieve their goals because they never took action. It does no good to have the previous seven steps eloquently written with a perfect plan if you never take action. Little actions, small accomplishments, and achieving milestones build momentum. Momentum is what will drive you toward finishing your goal. If you want to run a marathon, you must go for that first walk, jog, or run. I see people every day who have the talent and ability to achieve their dreams and goals. The problem is they never took action!

2. ***Cross it off.*** Check off all your milestones, both small and large. You will feel the momentum, and it feels invigorating as you move forward.

Step 6: Follow Up and Do Something Every Day

Follow up and do something every day to move toward your goal/dream. One of my favorite leadership lessons is:

What the boss checks gets done

and what the boss don't check doesn't get done.

You are the boss of your own goals—check them daily and follow up. Many people take action, but they never follow up. This is the reason why New Year's resolutions never work. People start with action on January 1, but they are not consistent. You must be consistent throughout the duration of your timeline from start to finish of your goal. If your goal is to get a master's degree, you can't stop and quit after your second year of undergraduate school. So many people focus so hard on the goal and talk themselves out of it because it seems too distant and unattainable. You must be consistent and do something toward your goal each and every day. If you're preparing to run a marathon four months from now, for example, make sure every day you are doing something to prepare yourself—you're riding a bike, swimming, jogging, running, doing physical therapy, stretching, doing strength cardio....

Write down what's in it for you, what you want out of this—do you want to lose weight, get the finisher's jersey, wear the medal, fit better in your clothes, feel better about yourself, have more confidence, visualize what it's going to be like when you're finished? Take a moment and think about the joy you're going to have when this is all finished.

You need a clear mental picture of this end state of your goal. When I was training to run my first marathon, I visualized crossing the finish line over and over and over, every day. When I was training, I visualized crossing the finish line and receiving my finisher's medal. When I did the thirty-day hot yoga challenge, all I thought about was how I would feel afterward.

The Myths about Goal Setting

We all need lots of powerful long-range goals to help us past the short-term obstacles.

Jim Rohn

Most college graduates will complete their education without ever receiving any instruction on how to set a goal. Goal setting is the most important skill you will ever acquire in your life.

We know the importance of becoming a member of the goal-setting three-percent club, so why do ninety-seven percent of the people still not have any written goals?

According to Brian Tracy, world-renowned expert in time management and goal setting, there are five reasons why people don't set goals:

1. *I already have goals*

   These are the people who have goals like *I want to go on vacation, I want to this and that*—these are all wishes, fantasies, hopes, and dreams with blank checks. *I want to* is not a goal, and if the goal is not in writing, it's just a vague wish.

2. *I don't need them*

   Saying that you don't need goals is like driving down the road with no road signs and no directions—you are just hoping for the best!

3. *I have everything all in my mind*

   The average person has 1,500 thoughts in a minute of stream of consciousness. The mind varies with the rapid thought all day long. When I first started going through cancer treatment, I had about 5,000 thoughts a minute streaming through my mind.

The ability to write down my goals and milestones in my journal helped me to clear my mind.

4. *I don't know how to set goals*

As previously stated, most college graduates will graduate with a degree but without a skill. Skills such as time management, resiliency, and goal setting are learned through practice. Follow the steps in this chapter, and you will be in the top three percent with clear goals and ready for success.

5. *Goals just don't work—life is unpredictable*

You can see where this is going. Without having a written goal, your life will continue to be unpredictable. Well-written goals are a roadmap for predictability and success.

You Have Two Choices in Your Life

You don't have to be great to start, but you have to start to be great.

Zig Ziglar

You can work on your own goals or work on someone else's goals, hopes, and dreams.

By writing goals, you can take control of your own life. I love the quote above; it's the perfect mantra for your confident psyche when it comes to actually putting goals down on a piece of paper.

At the beginning of this chapter, I listed eight specific goals that I set for myself after I was diagnosed with cancer on May 10, 2010. I set these goals at various times after my diagnosis, and I followed the nine steps that I have given you here in this chapter for goal setting. Let's see where I am on each one of these goals:

Cancer-free by January 2011 (Goal set May 2010): My surgeon, Dr. Lisa Shnayder, conducted surgery on my neck after a PET scan showed a potential cancerous spot in my lymph node area where the original tumor is located. In January 2011, Dr. Shnayder removed thirteen lymph nodes around the tumor spot, which were dissected and came back benign. This was a miracle in itself based on the size of the tumor, the initial diagnosis, and where I was in May 2010.

As I found my silence, I was able to "turn it all off" while going through radiation and chemotherapy. The more I was able to establish coping ways to relax and let it go, the more I felt the cancer leaving my body. I distinctly remember the day in week four that my radiologist, Dr. Kumar, grabbed a bunch of the medical students to take a look through the NG tube at my tumor. Dr. Kumar said, "The tumor is literally disappearing before my eyes every day. I've never seen a tumor disappear that fast." I already knew this: I had already felt the cancer leaving my body two weeks before he made that comment.

Living in Germany by December 2011 (Goal set June 2010): I set this goal of living in Germany while I was going to radiation treatment and was able to finally find my happy place—back in Germany where I was a second lieutenant. I set a clear goal with a deadline of how I could achieve it, then organized the plan. I took action, and I was able to get a job working in Stuttgart, Germany. I started work and arrived in Germany on August 1, 2011.

Run my first half-marathon by December 2011 (Goal set May 2010): I ran my first half-marathon in Munich, Germany in October 2011.

Run my first full marathon by June 2012 (Goal set May 2010): I ran my first full marathon in Hamburg, Germany in April 2012.

Run my fifth marathon by December 2014 (Goal set October 2011): I ran my fifth marathon in October 2014 in Munich, Germany and ran my eighth in Hamburg, Germany in April 2015.

Write my first book by January 2015 (Goal set August 2012): My first book is a learning experience, and I have adjusted my goal several times as I learn the process of writing, rewriting, and editing my first book. The book was completed in April 2015.

Start my speaking business by January 2015 (Goal set August 2012): Established Greg Cheek Speaks, LLC in July 2014.

Lose forty-five pounds by December 2013 (Goal set December 2012): Lost fifty-five pounds and now I'm down to the same weight I was when I was enlisted in the Air Force. The weight was lost, even though my saliva glands were severely damaged and my thyroid was destroyed during radiation therapy. I'm healthier and more fit now than I have been at any other time in my life. This was the ultimate example of backward planning and goal setting.

Goal-Setting Routine

The big secret in life is that there is no big secret. Whatever your goal, you can get there if you're willing to work.

Oprah Winfrey

You need to get in the habit of a goal-setting routine. Your routine can come from personal experience, mentors, or listening and studying various motivational speakers. I've been a vivacious listener of motivational speakers and their goal setting techniques since my youth when I first discovered Earl Nightingale and Zig Ziglar.

Develop your personal list of go-to goal-setting motivational mentors. My list includes the speakers that get me excited and fired up about my daily goals. Remember we are constantly writing, rewriting and shaping our current goals and those dreams! These speakers fire me up and they focus on goal setting, motivation, and resiliency: Jim Rohn, Og Mandino, General Colin Powell, LTG Calvin Waller, Zig Ziglar, Tony Robbins, Max Cleland, Dr. Martin

Seligman, Jack Canfield, John Wooden, Stephen Covey, Ray Lewis, Wayne Dyer, Dr. Deepak Chopra, Joyce Myers, Les Brown, Earl Nightingale, Eric Thomas, Ray Lewis, Vince Lombardi, and Jim Valvano.

Add your personal list, and don't forget about the mentors you can get by reading nonfiction motivational books. Stay motivated and attack all those goals and dreams!

Action

Daily goal setting and subconscious execution

Daily goal setting allows your subconscious mind to work in the present tense. Write down one new goal in your journal every morning. Start off the page with *My Goals* and put each daily goal, with today's date, in the present tense.

Do not look at your written goals from the previous day. You will notice the goals have been completed subconsciously while you were sleeping. Without you even having to think about it, the goals will begin to disappear off your list in your journal. At the end of the month, you can go back and take a look at the previous thirty days and look at the thirty goals that were completed. You'll be surprised how many goals you were able to complete!

Raise the ceiling

We discussed raising the ceiling in this chapter. This is powerful! In the good nature of taking massive action! Let's give this a quick shot right now.

Pick a goal and raise the ceiling one level. I will give you an example of what I did with my goal of a half-marathon. I moved to Germany in August 2011 and had never run more than ten miles. I initially decided to run the Munich half-marathon in October 2011. I challenged myself and raised my half-marathon expectation two levels. My first-level goal was to run my first full marathon in April 2012. My second-level goal was to run five marathons before my five-year cancer-free date. This means I would run five marathons in less than the next four years. I did not settle for just a half-marathon, which I enjoyed in Munich; I also ran that Hamburg marathon in April 2012, and I completed my seventh marathon a full eight months before my five-year checkup.

I would like you to do the same. Pick a goal, raise the ceiling one level, and tell me how it works. Contact me, and share your success on my website and the Three Points of Contact community.

Key Points

- Keep your goals in your journal for maximum success
- Always raise your goals one level
- Set deadlines, be optimistic, and create a network of support
- Find a mentor—could be motivational speakers or a support group

VISUALIZATION

Chapter Seven

Establish Trust and Belief in Yourself!

He who does not trust enough will not be trusted.

Lao Tzu

The Connection between Trust, Belief, and Being Happy

To be trusted is a greater compliment than being loved.

GEORGE MCDONALD

Happy, enthusiastic, successful, proactive, and energetic people have an innate ability to feel the law of belief or law of attraction—and they trust people. Research shows that satisfaction in life, career, and relationships is all directly tied to trust and belief. I recently read an article by an incredible young lady, Luminita D. Saviuc. At the get-go, "Fifteen Powerful Things Happy People Do Differently" discusses trust versus doubt. She states, "I equate happy with energetic, enthusiastic, cheerful, and many other emotions." Luminita suggests that happy people trust themselves and the people around them. Whether they are talking to a custodial person or the CEO of a billion-dollar company, somehow they seem to make the people they're interacting with feel as if there's something unique and special about them. They understand that beliefs are self-fulfilling prophecies.

I trust everybody…you will have to prove to me otherwise to gain my distrust!

That simple characteristic has taken the burden off my shoulders of judging everybody and every situation. In order for you to be in line with the law of belief—that is, whatever you believe with feeling and conviction becomes your reality—you must have trust. If you have a life filled with mistrust, then your law of belief will be circled around mistrust, and you must overcome this.

The time for trust and the law of belief is now, which run side-by-side. The law of belief is whatever you believe with feeling and conviction becomes your reality. It will not be until you change your beliefs that you begin to change reality and move forward and achieve your dreams.

Before the law of belief, let's discuss trust.

Trust

You must trust and believe in people or life becomes impossible.
Anton Chekov

Optimistic and happy people trust others and have impeccable trust in self. People want to be around others who can be trusted. This trait is a self-determined act in these unique behaviors that triggers a sense of happiness in yourself and in others around you. In any situation, distrust will close all interpersonal contact with any individuals outside your circle of trust. This will also destroy your chances of making new friends and creating healthy and happy relationships. You must trust yourself before you trust others and finally others will trust you.

University of California researcher Sonia Lubomski states that forty percent of our capacity for happiness is within our power to change. The development of trust is always one of the key factors in why people are happy or unhappy.

Alan Hall of Forbes wrote an article titled "I'm Out of Here! Why Two Million Americans Leave Their Job Every Month." One of the top factors was inability to trust in others. People do not trust the employer will take care of their needs, and they do not trust the boss.

Trust is in a decline in our society. We don't trust the workplace, relationships, friends, strangers…. Everywhere you turn, a lack of trust is rampant in our society. However, all statistical data and research provides inclusive evidence that in order for people to be happy, they must trust in themselves and in others.

I've served the better part of my life in an institution in the US Armed Forces that has an extremely high measure of trust. In a recent Gallup poll that rates the professional trust of institutions by the American people, the top institution again this year is the United States military—and it has been the top institution in trust since 1998.

What are the reasons that the military has received such high marks in trust by the American people? The obvious reason lies in trustful responsibility. The commissioned and noncommissioned officers of the armed forces are responsible for the sons and daughters of the United States during peace and war. These senior military personnel are responsible for the well-being and health of their troops, and ensuring they make it home safely.

No bigger trust in the world can be bestowed on any officer or noncommissioned officer than ensuring that our nation's sons and daughters are prepared to defend this country against all enemies, foreign and domestic.

Based on my research and experience as an enlisted airman in the United States Air Force and officer in the United States

Army, I wanted to look at the key factors that distinguish the military in the area of trust from the rest of society. I conducted interviews and research in each of the five branches of the United States military: I queried the United States Army, United States Marine Corps, United States Air Force, United States Navy, and United States Coast Guard. I researched the core values of each of the five branches of military and examined the common threads in regards to trust characteristics.

Five core values common to all five branches of the military support trust. I found all five to be critical in the areas of trust.

Before others can trust you and you can trust anyone else, you must trust yourself.

The following are a combination of the five common core values that will assist you in building trust in yourself.

Five Common Core Values in Building Trust

Honor

Life every man holds dear; but the dear man holds honor far more precious dear than life.

William Shakespeare

This is arguably the top trait when it comes to military core values. You don't lie, cheat, or steal, and you're accountable for your actions. You hold others accountable for their actions. When you say you're going to do something, you do it. If you have an appointment and you are required to be present somewhere, you are on time. We have a great saying in the military:

To be early is to be on time, to be on time is to be late, and to be late is wrong.

You could go a long way toward trust by just working on your honor:

honoring yourself and honor in the way you treat others.

Integrity

With integrity, you have nothing to fear, since you have nothing to hide. With integrity, you will do the right thing, so you will have no guilt.

Zig Ziglar

Integrity and trust are closely linked and one cannot exist without the other. Integrity is inherently established in the military and athletic culture—situations where competition, survival, success, and failure are created in very tight quarters over a sustained period of time. Trust is built in these situations over proven integrity and time. Go watch a group of military basic trainees at the start of basic training and then visit them after graduation in a mere two months. Amazing transformation is created by the cadre at the basic training locations! The trainees are put into daily and hourly situations so they can develop trust in each other.

Integrity forges that initial long-term trust!

Integrity is simply doing the right thing when no one is looking. Control your impulses and appetites; be responsible. You have the openness to be looked at and you have self-respect. Your bond is your word—when you say you're going to do something, you do it. People can trust you.

Courage
Courage is fear holding on a minute longer.
General George S. Patton

My research found this to be a key component and leading factor in establishing and maintaining trust. Courageous trust begins when you make the decision to become part of the military. You realize the decision you're making will require you to do a series of activities and events that will require stepping outside your comfort zone. The following is a list of the characteristics you build while serving in the armed forces that build courage and foster trust.

1. ***Dream Big!*** The entire experience of military service gives you confidence that you can achieve any goal and dream big.
2. ***Totally Committed.*** You learn what it's like to be fully engaged and throw yourself into an activity or task one hundred percent. Willingness to take risks and accept failure and try, try again until you succeed.
3. ***Move out of Your Comfort Zone.*** You boarded a plane and headed to basic training. This is just the beginning of long list of activities that require you to be accustomed to change and occasional discomfort. Courageous people learn to be resilient, risk failure, and understand that in order to succeed, you must also fail. Many people go through their entire life never leaving a comfort zone and live life in a rut. You cannot build trust, courage, and succeed with your big goals by playing it safe.
4. ***Courageous People Are Persistent.*** You are dared by the cadre to quit once you arrive at basic training. However, it's

engrained in you to never give up. Refuse to quit and you will eventually succeed.

Ductus Exemplo

I'm not scared of very much. I've been hit by lightning and been in the Marine Corps for four years.

Lee Trevino

I've served in the military since I was eighteen years old, in every position from garrison to combat. I've taught college classes to military personnel for nearly two decades. I've had the honor of spending a significant amount of time with every branch of the service in varied situations.

I see the commitment and dedication of our sons and daughters in uniform, family members, and Department of Defense civilians. The classes are always packed with insurmountable professionalism! These individuals lead by example in their actions. I've never seen a group of students so eager to learn. Our service members will always have my heart, and they make teaching seem like a vacation. This is my love and passion—teaching, coaching, and mentoring.

All the branches of the service are significant and absolutely amazing in what they do.

I never served in the Marine Corps, but there's an obvious difference between a Marine and anybody else (and not just military, but civilians, too). *Ductus Exemplo* means lead by example. It doesn't matter if I see a Marine in my college classroom, in a department store, in combat, in the airport, in garrison maneuvers, or in church…Marines lead by example. The Marine creed is *semper fidelis*, meaning always faithful—and that's about as trustworthy as you can get. I've never lived *Ductus Exemplo*, but I do know this: For my last thirty-five years of working with the military, when I see a service member, that is somebody I know I can trust.

Selfless Service

To me, teamwork is the beauty of our sport, where you have five acting as one. You become selfless.

Mike Krzyzewski

Selfless service is a service that is performed without any expectation of result or award for the person performing it.

This means service before self.

You have discipline and self-control. Put the welfare of the nation, the Army, and your subordinates before your own. Selfless service is larger than just one person. In serving your country, you are doing your duty loyally without thought of recognition or gain.

You control self-pity, anger, and frustration, and you have the determination to see a job through until it's finished. Anyone wearing a military uniform is demonstrating selfless service by putting the needs of their country before the needs of self. It's not uncommon in the holidays to see service members volunteering and doing things within the community for the homeless, disadvantaged, disabled veterans, or others.

The Law of Belief

Think you can, think you can't, either way you're right.

Henry Ford

Henry Ford did not come from a background of family with money and never got past the sixth grade. He simply had the belief that he could carry out his idea of producing mass production cars that would be inexpensive enough for the average person to afford. He believed this and became one of the most successful business-men of all time.

Everybody has heard somebody say, "I will believe it when I see it—and until I see it I won't believe it." These types of beliefs will keep you from your success and striving toward the future. Every time I've had success, I truly believed that I was going to do it—and when I believed I wasn't going to do something, I didn't do it.

In high school, I had a horrible feeling that I might fail that government class my senior year and not graduate. I had self-limit-ing thoughts in believing that I couldn't do something, and that's exactly what happened. When I believe I will do something, it happens. You can do anything you want to do! If you believe this, it will become your reality.

Four steps to focus and establish your law of belief:

Frequency: The more times that you see yourself with your goal and dream, the clearer and sooner law of belief will arrive.

Duration: The longer you can focus on the mental image of your goal and end state, the quicker you will arrive at success. Initially, you will focus for a few second bursts. With practice, you will focus for minutes at a time. The longer the better!

Clarity: The clearer the image you maintain will establish how quickly you establish your law of attraction. Practice, prac-tice, practice clarity to get the clearest and most vivid picture possible.

Intensity: The amount of emotion will increase the intensity and make the visualization much clearer, and the law of attraction will soon come true. It's an equal balance. Maintain your intensity with a calm nerve. Stay on point with the clear picture and don't pressure yourself; the law of belief will come with the universe.

Action

I believe in you!

My father gave me the greatest gift anyone could give another person: he believed in me.

Coach Jim Valvano

Begin to believe today that you are destined to be successful in whatever areas you desire. Get clear and focused on your true desires, make plans to achieve them and then believe, with absolute conviction, that you *will* achieve them. The universe will conspire to help you achieve it—once you believe it!

1. Write down five people you believe in who might need a push of encouragement. Send each person a hand written note or e-mail today and tell them all that you "believe in them." These three words are powerful and can change one life and the entire world. See how wonderful you feel after this little activity.

2. Write down the five reasons you believe in yourself—and write these five reasons everywhere! Put these five reasons somewhere you can see them. Share these reasons with your family and friends. You have everything in you to achieve every dream you desire! I believe in you, and believe in yourself!

The thirty-three percent rule!

This activity will help you connect to your law of belief and build trust with mentors, peers, and people to assist. You will need help from all directions in your life to achieve the law of belief. There is a direct link between your universal law of belief, mentors, and trust. These three together are extremely powerful. You need to get used to dividing your life into thirds (thirty-three percent).

Spend thirty-three percent of your time with people who need your help, trying to get where you are now. Coach, teach, and mentor these people. Give them thank you cards, write letters of recommendation, or fill out customer service cards. Pay something forward for them.

Spend thirty-three percent of your time with people who are at your level. These are colleagues, peers, and associates. You need this time together, and this is good networking. If you find that all your contacts and mentors are in this group (many of you will), you need to get out.

Spend thirty-three percent of your time with people who are above you. This is where you want to be, and don't be afraid to go to the top. You should be a bit uncomfortable with this group as they may be ten to twenty years ahead of where you are now. This uneasiness is amazing for your visualization of your dreams and linking those with the law of belief. That law of belief becomes much clearer when you are in contact with your mentor for that position. This is called the 10X rule. Find someone 10X ahead of where you are at this moment.

Try the thirty-three percent rule in your life for seven days and see what happens. You should see harmony in your life as you start putting the puzzle together of all three pieces to your personal pie. Remember to log all your findings in your journal.

Key Points

- Trust, belief, and being happy are all interconnected
- To be happier, trust others
- Be honorable and have integrity as your core values
- Be courageous and selfless
- If you believe it, it will happen!

VISUALIZATION

Chapter Eight

Resilient as a Duffel Bag

Never bend your head. Always hold it high.

Look the world straight in the eye.

HELEN KELLER

8

The Duffel Bag

I have a lot of stamina and I have a lot of resilience.
                                                    Hillary Clinton

The ever-durable and resilient duffel bag has a varied historical background, from the folklore of A.B. Patterson to nineteenth-century Prussian soldiers who carried all their possessions in a duffel (at this time named just "swag"). Whether named swagman, swag, or Matilda, it's known today as the ever-ready and sturdy duffel bag.

The Army and Air Force refer to this important initial item at basic training as the duffel bag. Seamen and Marines often refer to the duffel as sea bags. You can go to any surplus store today and find a duffel bag from the 1940s that will seemingly look brand-new. My first duffel from basic military training in 1980 in San Antonio is as sturdy and resilient as it was the day I received it. I've incorporated the duffel into my Three Points of Contact strategy with thirty-five years of resilient experiences.

My Own Duffel Bag

Success is the result of perfection, hard work, learning from failure, and persistence.

General Colin Powell

My thoughts strayed for a moment as I processed basic military training at Lackland AFB, TX. The week prior, I was 1,700 miles west in Sacramento, eighteen years old, my entire world in my backpack.

My first item of issue was the large extremely durable green canvas sack called a duffel bag. Wow! I can put four rucksacks in this duffel bag! My instructors yelling "Hurry up! Look straight! Move, move, move!" didn't faze me at all. I embraced the verbal barrage of "welcome to military life" mentorship and discipline. I was walking down the issue line and receiving brand new socks, pants, shirts, jackets—it was amazing!

I realized at this very moment that I had an opportunity in the US Air Force to better my situation for the rest of my life. That duffel bag would become my source of resilience for the next thirty-five-plus years. This entire book is a collection of tools of resiliency, and I hope you can put them all to use.

When the Lock on the Duffel Bag Breaks

It is hardly possible to build anything if frustration, bitterness, and a mood of helplessness prevail.

Lech Walesa

I was teaching an Introduction to Public Speaking course at the University of Nevada, Las Vegas (UNLV). This was an off-campus course offered in North Las Vegas adjacent to the Las Vegas Police Department. This type of non-traditional platform has always been exhilarating for me. My style is to teach classes on nights, weekends, remote locations, from the back of a tank three kilometers from the DMZ in South Korea, to a penitentiary in Kansas City, and everywhere in between. Give me a student looking for a chance and I will be there.

Changing people's ability to effectively communicate can change their entire life! My typical extended learning collegiate class is made up of students working multiple jobs, single parents, working parents, and every student in between with a dream. The dream in many cases is to just start college, and I convince them through effective communication mastery you can achieve any dream, including a college education. These are my students...now over 2,000 strong all over the world!

Manuel was one of my students at the off-campus UNLV site. Manuel came from Mexico and was the first in his entire family tree to attend college. I got to know him outside the classroom as he worked as a dishwasher at the Hard Rock Café. I liked to go there for lunch and grade papers and listen to the great music. Manuel and I would talk, and I got the opportunity to know this bright young man away from academia. Manuel was energetic, enthusiastic, confident, and full of goals, dreams, and aspirations. I knew he had difficulties back home as he sent money to help his family, worked three jobs, and carried a full load of classes. I felt a little bit of his emotional distress in his speeches and our personal conversations. His physical, spiritual, and family well-being seemed stable despite the weight he carried every day on his shoulders.

Six weeks into the semester, Manuel disappeared. My students know they can contact me 24/7. I never received a phone call, e-mail, or any type of message explaining Manual's sudden absence. I went to the Hard Rock Café to see him, but his manager said he hadn't been to work in a week. I asked if anyone had gone to check on him, and the manager said with a stern and irritating tone: "No." The manager conveyed to me that this was not his problem.

In the military, we take care of each other and I treat my students like my soldiers—we are family. My over 2,000 graduates of a Cheek Speaks class or a college class, you are my alumni, and I'm always available to you until I depart this earth. My leadership side of the situation told me something definitely wasn't right. Manuel told me he lived in the apartments behind the Thomas and Mack Center on the main campus of the University of Nevada Las Vegas.

I immediately went over to the apartments, asked around, and found where he lived. I knocked and knocked and knocked, but nobody came to the door. Ever persistent, I started to knock on the window of this small studio apartment...and finally Manuel answered. I looked Manuel directly in the eyes. He looked like a ghost, like he had not slept in a week. Manuel looked through me without acknowledgement. I looked over his shoulder, and on the table was a gun, box of ammunition, and a rope slung over the chair. I asked him to please come with me and talk at the In-N-Out Burger on the other side of campus.

I spent six hours that evening with Manuel, five of which were spent listening to him tell me everything he had to say. He let it all off his chest and I listened to it all—the sexual and physical abuse, the recent loss of his father and illness of his mother, the prospect of him quitting his college dream and returning to Mexico to support five other siblings, and a list of other stressful complications. Since Manuel did not have any medical insurance, I contacted a friend of mine who is a military mental health specialist, and we got Manuel some immediate In-N-Out counseling on the spot! Manuel went on to graduate from UNLV with a bachelor's degree, and he finished his MBA at University of New Mexico.

Resiliency is not just an issue for the military, fire department, or police department...it is an issue for everybody! Anybody can get to the point where the rubber band is about to break. If you think the rubber band is going to snap or the lock on the duffel is about to break, please reach out to others.

According to the Veterans Administration, Defense Department, Iraq and Afghanistan Veterans of America (IAVA), as of December 2014, an average of twenty-two veterans commit suicide every day. Veterans returning to civilian life are committing suicide at three times the rate of those remaining on active duty. For youth between the ages of ten and twenty-four, suicide is the third leading cause of death in the US with an average of 4,600 a year. Eighty-one percent of suicide deaths in this age range are males.

What do you do when the lock on the duffel bag breaks? Resilience can stretch like a rubber band, and like that lock, it can eventually break. The ability to be resilient is a learned activity. It is not enough to just put your head down and grind it out. The statistics at the beginning of this section are alarming. The ability to be resilient is required everywhere for everyone from teens to adults. The breakdown in being resilient can happen to anybody, no matter your financial makeup or your apparent life security—as we found out with the suicide of Robin Williams. Resilient as a duffel bag is about a set of tools that you place in your duffel bag. Applying these actions will prepare and protect you in upcoming resilience situations.

Resiliency Works: A Lifetime of On-The-Job Experience

I still have highs and lows, just like any other person. What's missing is the lack of control over the super highs, which became destructive, and the super lows, which are immediately destructive.

Patty Duke

Several lifetimes' worth of resilience experience are stuffed into my trusted duffel bag. It seemed that the diagnosis of cancer was verification and definitely a test of my resilience. You're told during cancer treatment to not let the "highs get too high" and the "lows get too low."

The ups and downs are so frequent between scans, and watching the lab numbers is like riding a daily and sometimes hourly emotional roller coaster. White blood cell counts are too high, red blood cell counts are too low, platelets are below 50,000, and you're losing weight too fast. There is always something going on. Forget the advice of regulating your emotions and not letting the "highs get too high" and the "lows get too low." When you are feeling great and you are having one of those "I can conquer this, I can do anything" moods, embrace it and love it. Believe me, the cancer cells don't like your happiness! Get out and scream, dance, and do whatever you want to spill emotions in the good times.

You must moderate this behavior in thinking if you get too high, you will fall way too low! I will take the high feeling and deal with the lows, as I know they are coming too. This was new to me, because if I have had a great experience in life, I let it go, and if I have an experience that is low, I monitor the low to ensure I quickly bounce back. You must always have your hand in your duffel bag when you're going through difficulties in life. All cancer patients know one striking fact: every time you go to an appointment, you are thirty seconds away from great news or really bad news.

I arrived at my six-month follow-up appointments in the highest spirits of my life. I felt great, fantastic, strong, and I breezed through the first three appointments on that chilly morning. My blood work, dental, and radiation follow-ups all went perfectly. I was hugging everybody, high-fiving, and was on top of the world. I had one appointment left with my surgeon, Dr. Shnayder, my otolaryngologist, who serves as the lead of my amazing medical support team. In the previous six months, every time I saw Dr. Shnayder, she would enter the room with a big smile and ask how I was doing. We would embrace the amazing progress that had taken place in the past several months.

This visit was different. As soon as Dr. Shnayder walked in the room, I could notice the seriousness on her face. I knew something was wrong and I immediately started talking—and talking a lot. It's a nervous habit of mine, and I would not stop and Dr. Shnayder listened intently as she sensed I knew something was wrong. Dr. Shnayder looked me in the eyes and said:

"We might have a small situation. Your Positron Emission Tomography/Computed Tomography (PET) scan came back showing a potential hotspot on one of your lymph nodes."

For anyone who has been in a similar uncomfortable predicament, you know your mind races. I didn't hear anything Dr. Shnayder said after hearing "small situation." I didn't completely comprehend what that meant, but I could tell by the staid look on Dr. Shnayder's face that this was serious.

Dr. Shnayder recommended that we do surgery and take the lymph nodes out that were located around the tumor location. The next step was to dissect each lymph node—that was the only way to reveal the truth about this suspicious lymph node. Dr. Shnayder said, "I have a feeling the hot lymph node is due to calcification during the radiation process, but I won't know for sure until I go in there and take the lymph nodes out."

Three weeks later, thirteen lymph nodes were removed via surgery and dissected. The final report revealed no cancer cells inside the lymph nodes. I didn't realize it at the time, but I had reached a graduate level assurance and understanding of resiliency. In medical terms, I was unofficially cancer-free.

In my mind, I was officially cancer-free months ago!

One month before this emotional and trying six-month checkup, I was selected to attend the Master Resiliency Training (MRT) at the University of Pennsylvania. Dr. Karen Reivich, co-author of *The Resilience Factor* and research associate of the Positive Psychology Center at the University of Pennsylvania, hosted the training.

I was so keyed up from the MRT that I breezed through the potentially devastating news from Dr. Shnayder without a resilient hitch. The training at the University of Pennsylvania is cutting-edge and state-of-the-art in the field of human positive performance. The training assisted me by putting up my resilient shield from my past experiences and the recent training with Dr. Karen Reivich.

I'm reading my journal notations from December 2010 as I sit on the steps adorning the Notre Dame in Paris, France. The pages seem to flow smoothly from the lymph node diagnosis by Dr. Shnayder up to the surgical date in January 2011. The days synchronized in harmony...it was like clockwork.

I meticulously and subconsciously eased through all the steps I learned from MRT, seemingly in the shadows of Dr. Martin Seligman, the world's most renowned educator in the study of learned optimism.

- Hunt the "good stuff" every day or look for the good in life around me—it's everywhere!
- Focus on increasing increased my self-confidence and rely on my strong relationships.
- Avoid *all* catastrophic (end-of-the-world) thinking, manage my highs and lows, and maintain my positive emotions, and watch that I don't fall into depression.

The training at the University of Pennsylvania was amazing! I didn't realize until afterward that I moved subconsciously through all these steps.

So yes, resiliency absolutely works!

Your Basic-Issue Duffel Bag

I pieced together my Three Points of Contact resilience areas and the duffel bag metaphor upon a lifetime of experiences. The experiences include enlisted and commissioned military service with a tour in combat, a graduate degree in speech communication, seventeen-plus years as a speech and interpersonal communication college professor, two years' research for this book, amazing training at the University of Pennsylvania's Master Resiliency Training program, and finally, my ultimate resilient final exam against cancer.

Please go through this book and find items that you like and place them in your duffel bag, rucksack, or anywhere else in your life—please use them. Remember to keep one hand on the wheel and one hand on your duffel bag.

Imagine you are in line at resiliency basic training. The following six areas will be placed in your duffel bag and are your initial issue. Keeps these by your side and use all six every day.

1. Hunt the good stuff
2. Practice makes self-confidence perfect
3. Build strong and meaningful relationships
4. Never stop chasing your dreams
5. Beware of catastrophic thinking
6. Leverage your energy resilience

Hunt the Good Stuff

A good school teaches resilience—the ability to bounce back.

Kate Reardon

Hunt the Good Stuff is an amazing activity taught by Dr. Karen Reivich at the Master Resiliency Training (MRT) at the University of Pennsylvania. The purpose of this daily activity is to enhance positive emotions, particularly in the area of being thankful. Research shows that individuals who routinely acknowledge and express thanks derive greater health benefits, sleep benefits, and relationship benefits.

Every day you are going to Hunt the Good Stuff and start your day by writing three in your journal. You will realize how important it is for your positive mentality to write down three positive events. This is the "glass half full" and "glass half empty" dilemma. Start each day with three good things that happened the day before, and your day is already off to a great start. I encourage you to follow the lead from MRT and have your colleagues, friends, and as many others as possible hunt and share the good stuff. You can join in and follow the entire worldwide Hunt the Good Stuff community at #HTGS.

Hunting the Good Stuff was a part of my daily ritual during cancer treatment; it became clear to me that composing my thoughts, ideas, feelings, and emotions was essential in confirming

my increased confidence and strengthened resiliency. You will immediately increase your level of success by adopting this simple
activity. Go Hunt The Good Stuff now!

Practice Makes Self-Confidence Perfect
*When you have confidence, you can have a lot of fun. And when you
have fun, you can do amazing things.*

Joe Namath

Belief in one's self is clearly apparent in resilient people and
ultimately leads to self-confidence.

Self-confident and resilient people have dreams and well-defined goals. You show me someone with clear, defined goals and
written dreams, and you will see a self-confident and successful
person.

The interesting thing about self-confidence is not whether
you achieve all your goals and dreams. It's the person you become
in the process. You become confident and proud, you stand tall,
and you look at yourself differently in the mirror. You learn your
strengths and weaknesses to successfully navigate day-to-day situations. Self-confidence attracts others and reinforces their success,
contributing significantly to their long-term resilience.

** My Separate Duffle Bag Cast Study at Lackland AFB, Texas
I conducted an informal study while I was in San Antonio attending my son's United States Air Force Security Forces Technical
School graduation at Lackland Air Force Base, Texas. I visited two
local recruiting stations in San Antonio and talked to recruits as
they were in the process of joining the military. I then went to the
base and asked questions to the airmen who had just started basic
training and were still in their civilian clothes, and finally to the

airmen who had recently graduated basic training and were attending technical training school at Lackland AFB.

What are your goals, dreams, and self-confidence levels? I then asked five basic questions that I learned in the Master Resiliency Training at the University of Pennsylvania. The questions addressed their current standing in the five areas of comprehensive fitness: social, spiritual, family, emotional, and physical. My final study observations looked like this:

1. The recruits still at the recruiting station had few goals and no dreams other than just joining the military. The recruits had very little if any self-confidence. This group was able to talk about, on average, one area of confidence in comprehensive fitness—normally family. The recruits didn't have a sense of emotional, physical, spiritual, or social well-being. This part of the study really resonated with me as I thought about sleeping on that recruiter's doorstep to get into the United States Air Force.

2. The recruits who had just arrived at Lackland Air Force Base now had a few short-term goals and every third airman had a dream. The self-confidence was greater than it was several weeks ago when they were at the recruiting station. The airmen were able to talk, on average, about three of the five areas of comprehensive fitness with confidence.

3. The third group of recruits had now graduated from basic training and was starting technical school with the United States Air Force security forces. These airmen were all extremely excited and motivated, had short-term goals, long-term goals, and dreams, and were able to talk about their

feelings on all five levels of comprehensive fitness. Their self-confidence was off the charts.

I conducted this study looking to track a theme of self-confidence as young people move from civilian life to the recruiter's doorstep to basic training to graduation. I found a clear link between the five levels of comprehensive fitness and goal setting as they link to the level of self-confidence.

Self-confident people have goals, dreams, and a solid foundation of what is taught at the University of Pennsylvania in the areas of social, spiritual, family, emotional, and physical needs. If you looked into the eyes of these young people, you could see that the difference two months can make from the recruiter station, to basic training, to technical training is absolutely amazing! I realized, that was me thirty-five years ago.

I would be remiss if I didn't mention one other thing that I noticed in my study of the over seventy-five airmen in my visit to San Antonio—the difference in happiness, enthusiasm, and determination; an absolute 180-degree difference between the two months from start to finish.

I truly thank all the airmen for their time and for participating in this study and deciding to serve our country. I wish all of them well and a bright and prosperous future.

Aim high!

U.S. AIR FORCE

Build Strong and Meaningful Relationships
Friendship is not something you learn in school. But if you haven't learned the meaning of friendship, you really haven't learned anything.

Muhammad Ali

To survive and prosper, you must have strong and meaningful relationships. These relationships are many and varied, and include all types of acquaintances. Resilient people have relationships that provide the appropriate reinforcement and support when required; they never judge anyone else, give themselves fully to each relationship, and reap the rewards of friendship. Listed below are more examples to help you build friendship.

Support Groups: These are fantastic. Support groups come in all capacities: writing groups, running groups, walking groups, Alcoholics Anonymous groups, fitness groups, bridge clubs, cancer support groups...the list goes on.

I attended the Support for People with Oral and Head and Neck Cancer (SPHONC) group at the University of Kansas Cancer Center. What an amazing group of people—and the group answered so many of my questions from firsthand experience. I strongly recommend attending one of these support groups. You'll find so much amazing information, support, new friends, and you'll develop trust and self-confidence.

Circle of Trust: This is a circle of friends that you can count on. Meet at your house or get together for a pizza. I had a group of friends that would get together at a pizza place and watch sports on the weekend together—this gives you an opportunity to socialize and get your mind off of cancer in another setting. Through one of my friends, I was introduced to Command Sergeant Major (CSM) Charles Ritchie. I met and spoke with CSM Ritchie one day after my diagnosis—and he was one year cancer-free. The one hour we spent together at a local restaurant was a tremendous help. I needed to talk to someone who had gone through a similar treatment that I was about to go to. I'm a big advocate for being part of a cancer support group to help others in similar situations.

Mentor: A mentor is a very important person in the resilient process—and, trust me, it's very nice to have one or two people in which you have complete confidence and trust—and someone you can bounce your thoughts and ideas off of.

BFF (*best friend forever*): This is extremely popular with teens and my college students. I think this is great—somebody you can go to directly and just chat. How many of us have a good friend who we can talk to for hours on end? In resilient times, this is a great relief.

Self: Just a reminder not to forget the relationship with the most important person—yourself. This would seem like common sense; however, when you get a resilient situation, just quiet yourself and don't forget about *you*.

Never, Ever, Ever Stop Chasing Your Dreams

If you don't know where you're going, you will probably end up somewhere else.

Laurence J. Peter

In the movie *Rudy*, Rudy's brother gives him a letterman's jacket from the University of Notre Dame for his birthday. Rudy tells his brother, "Thanks for believing in me. Nobody else does." His brother replies, "Dreams are what make life worth living."

Resilient people have dreams! Never stop chasing your goals. When you have a resilient event in your life, you will refocus your aspirations. When I was diagnosed with cancer, I realized that somewhere along the way I had stopped chasing my dreams.

I made the decision to go after my dreams of running a marathon, writing a book, and starting my speaking business. I've accomplished all those dreams and now I'm on to a new set of goals. You must live every day with complete passion and exuberance for life! Dream big, and remember…raise your goals two levels!

From the *Children of Sanchez*:

Take the crumbs from the strong soldiers and they won't die.

Beware of Catastrophic Thinking

Positive thinking will let you do everything better than negative thinking will.

Zig Ziglar

Catastrophic thinking is defined as contemplating about irrational worst-case scenarios. It can drive up your anxiety and completely freeze all actions and momentum. We've all had situations of catastrophic thinking—this is really a key area in maintaining your strong resiliency. We've all had the situation when we are given news and automatically think of the worst-case scenario.

When I was a captain teaching at the Academy of Health Sciences at Fort Sam Houston, Texas, I was ten minutes from giving a graduation presentation when I received a phone call from my wife that a routine x-ray on my young daughter Stefanie showed a spot on her lung. I could not stop thinking of the worst possible scenario…and my presentation was a disaster. I continued to spiral and catastrophize.

The radiologist found the negative of the x-ray was bad—Stefanie was okay. When a stressful situation happens, look at the worst-case scenario, the best-case scenario, then average the two out into the middle.

Don't immediately think the worst—be optimistic, develop positive pictorial visualization, and act with stillness and calm.

Leverage Your Energy Resilience

Your body has something in the neighborhood of forty trillion cells—quite a consulting committee. Call on it when you're confused or undecided. Relax quietly and ask your body what it has to say.

Victoria Moran

Manage your energy through a variety of strategies.

For energy resilience, meditate, control breathing, and focus on muscle relaxation. We must discuss the need for rejuvenation to maintain resilience and share strategies that can be used to re-energize ourselves.

My favorite rejuvenation strategies: prayer, exercise, activity, sleep, rest, relaxation, and laughter. The next step is to work on your controlled breathing and positive imagery. My example is the bliss and beauty I found in yoga. Yoga helped me become cancer-free through the use of stillness.

Leverage your stillness—this is your strength!

Action

Reflection

Reflect back on three difficult or negative experiences in your life.

Note what you've learned from overcoming and/or surviving these challenges. Which one of your six items in your initial issue duffel bag would have helped with these challenges?

Take a look at some of the other chapters in this book and what other ways you could have used these areas to help you with any difficult situation. Place these new items in your duffel.

Congratulations—you have just found additional items to put in your duffel bag to prepare for future situations that require you to be resilient.

Take it to a level ten every day

I've always used an activity taught by the famous and energetic motivational speaker Tony Robbins. Tony taught a numbering activity on a scale from one to ten. Simply take an initial number of what you give an activity and figure how to take it to the next level.

For example, I went for a run today—it would be a five on a scale of one to ten. However, if I added my headphones, I can make this a six. If I ran through the hills behind my house, I can make it a seven. If I ran intervals, I can make it an eight. If I want to make this run a ten, I would wear headphones, take the train to an unknown location, turn on my GPS, and run back to the house.

I want you to imagine that you're at the recruiting station in my story. The recruiting station in this case is going to be wherever you are today. Are you at work, on a plane, at home, at the gym? What is your number today on how you feel? How is your motivation? Your happiness? Look at your duffel bag and see what you can do to increase the activity you're doing. List everything you need to do to get yourself to that level ten today. How do you feel when you get there? Invincible, unstoppable, on top of the world? This activity increases my resiliency and energy, and I feel amazing.

Key Points

- Create your own duffel bag of tools
- If you feel stretched, reach out to others
- Find a positive experience at least three times every day
- Always practice your self-confidence
- Foster meaningful relationships
- Avoid negative thinking

ACTION

ACTION

ACTION

Chapter Nine

Make Plans to Travel Today

Don't tell me how educated you are; tell me how much you traveled.

Mohammed

9

Hands Down, I'm Alive Because of Travel!

To travel is to take a journey into yourself.

DANNY KAYE

"Greg, the biopsy confirmed that you have stage III cancer...."

I went blank for a minute as the blood rushed through my body. All I felt was cancer, death, cancer, death...I felt helpless, alone, and out of control. The doctor left the room as I waited for the nurse for following instructions.

I could feel a strong pull on my pride and determination.

I sat up in the bed, put my head up, and suddenly I could feel the thousands of friends I've met all over the world. My mind raced to Turkey, Korea, Germany, England, Japan, Saudi Arabia, Kuwait, Ireland, Scotland, and twenty-plus other countries and all fifty states. I remembered the friendship and stories of survival, strength, and the passion I'd heard from all around the world. I could see their faces, and I sensed their energy.

I've always said, "No matter the problem, I always have travel. The exuberance I gained from travel has helped me overcome anything. I can handle this." I sat up in the bed as the nurse arrived, and I was invigorated again with the idea of travel.

Two minutes after my diagnosis, I put cancer aside and focused on the positive I had in my life. I wasn't done traveling and seeing the rest of the world. Let's go!

Travel and Passport

Twenty years from now you will be more disappointed by the things you didn't do than by the ones you did do.

Mark Twain

I found it appropriate to write this chapter while I travel to another new destination. I departed my home in Stuttgart, Germany by train this morning to Budapest, Hungary. The beautiful train ride took me through Bavaria, Munich, Zurich, Salzburg, and finally to the amazing train station in historic Budapest.

I'm sitting in an amazing café in Budapest looking over the Danube River, the Buda Castle, and again I'm now completely energized. I was just asked by the waiter the same question that I've been asked almost daily since I was eighteen years old and boarded a plane for military basic training in San Antonio, Texas: "You seem to be very happy. You must be having a good day."

I responded, as I always do, "My life is a great one. Living is travel and travel is living!"

How could I not be happy after experiencing another day of stunning travel and living my Three Points of Contact lifestyle? I'm the happiest person in the world.

I boasted to the meticulous waiter about his friendly city. Hungary is one of the most beautiful countries I've ever traveled to—just breathtaking! Budapest is so clean, everyone is so proud of their country, and the architecture of this spectacular city is off the charts.

This is always the story when I travel. The travel can be to Gillette, Wyoming; Adana, Turkey; Dongducheon, South Korea; Alamogordo, New Mexico; or Riyadh, Saudi Arabia—people everywhere are amazing! Living a life of daily joy and happiness, although through a life with so many ups and downs, is a result of my passion and desire to travel and meet new people.

Don't let the evening news, the travel channel, people with rumors, or anyone else tell you how people live in Asia, Europe, South America, across your state, across the country, or anywhere else in the world. Ask questions, try different food, get off the main road, and people will astonish you. Get out and meet people everywhere, get a passport, and go see people across the globe. Travel will fill your soul with goodness. The stories of travel remain in my soul forever.

The excuses for putting off travel include cost, airfare, hotel, food, and every other reason and excuses why you can't—or shouldn't—travel. Always an excuse why someone can't do it today and another excuse to delay until next week, next month, next year, or in the distant future.

Stop making excuses, and set a time to get out there and travel! Networking with your friends, associates, relatives, and colleagues is the key to getting out and seeing the world. Everybody has a friend, relative, or colleague living somewhere in the next county, state, or country abroad. Get out there, enjoy it, and go see them. Do it for your health and well-being.

One Day Island

Travel is fatal to prejudice, bigotry, and narrow-mindedness, and many of our people need it sorely on these accounts. Broad, wholesome, charitable views of men and things cannot be acquired by vegetating in one little corner of the earth all one's lifetime.

Mark Twain

There is an actual place called One Day Island. It belongs to the residents of "I Will Travel One Day" and people who use that procrastinating and decaying word "tomorrow." The residents claim, "I can't do this today," "Tomorrow is too busy," and "I will go there in the future—One Day."

During cancer treatment, I was surrounded by long-time inhabitants of One Day Island. People telling me the woes of *I wish I did this, I wish I did that,* and *why did I wait until now to think about what I could have done.* This is the saddest place in the world to end up as a resident of One Day Island. Don't end up in a spot where you're sitting and wishing I would have, could have, and should have done this or that.

Upon my cancer diagnosis, the only thing I could think of was the places I still needed to see. I came up with a new list of travel destinations before I left the hospital after the biopsy and diagnosis. The Three Points of Contact immediately raised a temporary fence protecting me from the fear of the diagnosis. I put myself into a positive frame of mind. The **optimism** of travel and new adventure filled my thoughts, as did my **visualization** of getting there and finally planning the **action**. Cancer was already on its way out, and I only focused on the positivity of traveling the globe!

Two weeks after chemo, radiation, surgery, stomach PEG tubes, losing saliva glands, losing taste buds, and going through a difficult four months, I decided it was time to get back to my job (opportunity).

My position required lots of monthly travel, and my colleagues at Fort Leavenworth were extremely supportive throughout my entire treatment process. Every soldier and civilian at C Team, MCTP at Ft. Leavenworth provided amazing support and assisted me in getting back on the road.

The team traveled to Alaska, Hawaii, Colorado, Texas, and South Korea in the four months after treatment. Those four months of travel and being back with my colleagues saved my life! Getting away from the cancer center and the four walls of the house to travel to the northern lights in Alaska, North Shore Beach in Hawaii, Pikes Peak summit in Colorado, amazing Korean food and Seoul skyline, and visiting the friendly folks of Texas—it really gave me the break and boost I needed.

The travel placed cancer on the shelf, and I was back in my original state of traveling, talking, visiting…and most of all *living*. Everything I've been able to do in my life has always circled around the potentiality of travel now and in the future.

Dreaming of Travel

Remember that happiness is a way of travel, not a destination.
Roy M Goodman

My best friend Keith's father was a career airman in the United States Air Force. As a pre-teen, I'd listen to all his amazing stories of travel to exciting places. The presentation of the United States flag at a memorial service is one of the greatest duties bestowed on a military officer. I had the distinguished honor of presenting the United States flag to my best friend's mother, my second mother, Ms. Joan Kirksey, at the funeral for her husband, Tech Sergeant Walter Kirksey.

As a young US Army captain, I had now traveled the world several times and developed my rucksack full of stories by the time of Mr. Kirksey's passing. I stood as tall as I could and tried to touch the sky in my officer dress military uniform. I'd just received the flag from the honor guard as I gazed at the casket.

Seemed like yesterday he had encouraged me to try and enlist in the US Air Force after I failed to graduate high school. Now I was standing here as a US Army captain, wondering if I had thanked him enough for getting me to take action and encouraging me to enlist in the US Air Force. I pressed the colors to my heart as I looked at my grieving family and friends, and my mind drifted to the travel stories I had shared with my mentor.

Mr. Kirksey seemed to clash on and off with cancer, and the talk of travel kept him young and invigorated time and time again. His eyes ignited, and I noticed a renewed energy in his voice when we shared our now innumerable travel locations between the two of us. I held Old Glory tighter to my heart and I tried to control my emotion, as I would soon present the flag.

I've performed this important duty at least ten times in my career. This time, however, it was for my personal family and friends, and it was going to be very difficult to compose myself. Tears began to fall from my cheeks and landed on my airborne wings on my chest as I looked down at the crisp corners of the tightly folded flag from the honor guard. Thoughts of travel raced through my mind, combined with thoughts of a marriage to the love of his life and their four magnificent kids.

I handed the perfectly folded flag to Ms. Kirksey for honorable military service from a grateful nation.

During my cancer treatment, I shared similar stories of travel. I would stop, contemplate, and realize what Mr. Kirksey went through—and the reason he was able to fight cancer as long as he did was the exact reason I'm able to continue with such vivacity.

I've shared my travel exploits with others on a daily basis since my first trip to San Antonio and Lackland AFB. The combination of optimism, visualization, and action is a sum of travel.

Travel is the best cure for anything that ails.

Auf Geht's! (Time to Go, Move Out!)

Life is either a daring adventure or nothing.

Helen Keller

Time to stop talking and start moving.

You are about to embark on one of the healthiest activities in the world—travel! Get out and meet new people, experience cultures, and learn the language. You will be astonished—guaranteed!

Aldous Huxley stated, "Travel is to discover that everyone is wrong about other countries."

You will meet far more friendly people on the road than you ever will at home. Travelers are looking to share experiences with each other and give advice, tips, and recommendations, and point people in the direction of adventure and places to see. Get a new navigation system, backup map, and check out the back roads and enjoy yourself. You will find out that you return to work and tackle that next project. Travel reduces stress, and don't be surprised that you begin planning your next trip before you return.

Notate your experiences in your journal. Note your enjoyment, the people you met, and the cultures you enjoyed the most. Think about doing a travel blog to let your friends and family know how much fun you're having. Try to learn a couple words and phrases when you travel to another country. Before you depart, learn to say "hello," "how much," "please," "thank you," "my name is," "and how do you say this" in that country's language. This will go a long way toward ingratiating yourself to your new culture.

You will find that people from other countries outside of the United States are much more tolerant of the fact that you don't speak their language. Meet your new friends halfway, and they will bend over backward for you—and you now have friends for life. Get out there and enjoy yourself, then tell me about your travels on my website.

Have fun or *Viel Spaß!*

Action

1. Don't have a passport? You may not have a plan to travel now, but go get one now! Follow the link below to the US passport website. When the time arrives to travel abroad, you are ready.
   http://travel.state.gov/content/passports/english/passports.html

2. Contact friends living around the world and start networking and setting up your travel plans. Start with the United States and go abroad. You have one contact already:
   a. Greg Cheek, Author, *Three Points of Contact,* greg@gregcheekspeaks.com
   b.
   c.
   d.

3. Write a list of all the cities nearby and around the world you want to go visit. Visualize your travels there. Place your emotions and feelings into your vision. Prepare an action on your request. This is already done; get it on the calendar. Let's do this! I can't wait to hear about your travels.

Key Points

- Travel feeds the soul!
- Do not become a citizen of One Day Island
- Stop dreaming and start living—no more excuses!
- Network to start traveling across the globe
- Get your passport today and GO!

ACTION

Chapter Ten

Carry Your Ruck at All Times

I have a pro tools rig that I carry in my backpack.

WILL.I.AM

10

Just My Ruck, Please!

*I am much inclines to live from my rucksack, and let
my trousers frey all the like*

HERMANN HESS

I woke up groggy, the nasogastric tube tube still in my nose as I
looked up in a haze and tried to gather my thoughts and composure.

The doctor opened the curtain and squeezed himself inside
the small recovery area and quietly said, "I have the results of your
biopsy." I've seen that look on the doctor's face my entire life.

Immediately my mind began racing—the same way it did
when I was a second lieutenant during Operation Desert Storm.
The UH-1 helicopter crew chief shook me as I was in a deep slum-
ber on our way to a meeting in Safwan, Iraq. He screamed in my
ear, "Sir! We are going down! Put your head between your legs, we
are going down!" We were a couple thousand feet in the air, and I
could hear the engine struggle and I began to see flashes of my life.

The look from the doctor's eyes mirrored that of the crew chief
on that scorching afternoon as we crossed from Kuwait into Iraq...
the same look when the police came to my door as little kid to tell

me that my mom was in the hospital again...the same look when the high school counselor told me I failed my government class by one point my senior year, and I would not be able to graduate the next day with my friends...the same look when the Air Force recruiter told me I didn't qualify for initial entry into the US Air Force.

This is the look that nobody in the healthcare field wants to make, either. The doctor asked if I wanted any family here for the results of the biopsy. This news would not get better with time, I realized—my colleagues were on business in California, and I was in Kansas City alone—so I responded told him, "I'm okay; please tell me."

The doctor took a big gulp, looked at the ground to compose himself, and looked me in the eyes. "You have cancer. The lab results confirmed that you have a stage III tumor at the base of your tongue."

This was odd—I had throat cancer. I didn't chew tobacco, smoke, or even drink alcohol.

"I'm sorry," the doctor continued. "The nurse will be back in to give you your next instructions."

The nurse gave me my follow-up appointment for the next day. This appointment would determine the start of my post-cancer diagnosis azimuth.

I gathered myself, smiled, and thanked the nurse for the surgical biopsy procedure. I sensed the tension from the nurse as she was really speechless as she glanced at my results and instructions on the chart. I mentioned to the nervous nurse, "After a month of coughing up blood, I now at least have a direction to attack. Thanks, you are a wonderful nurse."

I looked around the floor by the bed. Where is it, where is it? Ahhhh, I found it!

All I need is my rucksack.

I got out of the hospital skivvies, put on my clothes, and slung the ruck over my back—just as I've done my entire life. I stood up tall and tried to look as confident as one can under the recent news.

I walked outside the hospital main entrance and sat under a tree.

I read several motivational quotes and wrote in my journal for twenty minutes. Pulled out my Ziploc bag of trusty thank you cards. I filled out two well-thought-out and heartfelt handwritten thank you cards—

One thank you card for the wonderful receptionist just inside the hospital entrance with the dream of going to college someday. I wanted to tell her that I'm a college communication professor, and I can detect the drive in someone's eyes. In bright red I wrote, "You have it, now go out there and get it...I believe in you!" I gave her the contact information to the admissions representative at Kansas City Kansas Community College where I've taught for many years.

The second thank you card was for the doctor that had the thankless task of delivering the bad news of my cancer diagnosis. I sent ten text messages to several family and friends simply saying, "Thanks for being there for me all these years," and "I love you." This always happens after thank you notes! I was completely energized after the forty-five minute reprieve.

After all, what can go wrong?

I've got my ruck!

What is a Ruck?

If you think about America, it is about getting your backpack on and heading out.

Nick Frost

A rucksack (ruck for short) is a term for a simple backpack, a knapsack, or a bergen, which is simply a sack with two straps.

This is a bag that will supply us with all of our essential items. The rucksack is a staple item in the military; as a soldier, I always have to have a rucksack.

My father and I got together for my eighteenth birthday. He explained to me the rules of our family. This tradition has been passed down from my grandfather to my father, and now I get to carry the guidon.

"Son," he said, "you now have three options when you finish high school: get a job, go to college, or join the military. But none of those options involves you living at home. You're out of high school, you're eighteen years old, and it's time to let your mother have her own life and you to become a man."

The day after I finished summer school (due to failing that American Government class my senior year), I packed my backpack with all my life possesions, and I took off for an adventure that still continues today. Every time a situation arises in my life and it's time to move out, I know that as long as I have my ruck, everything will be okay.

The beautiful thing about the Army is everybody has a ruck. I've been able to pick up ideas over the years from what I used as a kid with a backpack. The military has rucksacks for every occasion, for various missions and deployments.

We have rucks for special operations to include Navy SEALs, US Army Special Forces, Army Rangers, US Air Force Pararescue, and Marine Recon to logisticians, medics, service support personnel, and on and on. Over time, I've gotten efficient in having what I need to sustain myself in my ruck. Packing a ruck or a typical backpack is a tremendous skill and a technique you can use for the rest of your life. I've had some items for a long time and other items I picked up from being a keen traveler around the world. I hope you find these ruck tips useful and you can put these techniques to work right away.

This chapter will discuss the specific items for your ruck. In the military, we normally have an (A) bag for immediate use items and a (B) bag for long-term items or later on the trip. This is a bit of a different ruck.

Our ruck is made up of items that support the 12.5 ways in our Three Points of Contact. We will call this your Three Points of Contact ruck. The A items are quick-use and on hand for immediate use, and the B items are virtual, not exactly present, but needed in everyday life. Now, let's pack your ruck for success.

Three Points of Contact "A" Actual Ruck Items

Begin with a Journal

There are certain things that make me relax, like writing in my journal. That's the only time that I'm relaxing. It's the only time I really get to examine myself.

Jessica Simpson

Every successful person I've ever met kept a journal for notes, dreams, goals, and daily motivation. They may call the writing apparatus a different name, but they have some way of logging this information. Your ruck journal is for freeing your mind, benefiting your health, and allowing you to focus on positive activities. Write your own daily motivational notes. Write motivational notes to yourself during both the good and difficult times. You may have lots of items in your ruck, such as a cell phone, notebook, computer, and other tech items or even personal hygiene items. Nothing is more important in your ruck than your journal.

I learned many life lessons in all my days caddying at the country club from ages thirteen to seventeen. Caddying for Mr. Bob

Hope was my biggest honor. I noticed that he was writing in his journal throughout the entire round of golf. I asked, "Is everything okay?" He said that he was doing great—that he was just writing a note to himself to enjoy the moment and to call his dear friend who was ill. He told me that writing in a journal relaxes him and has always given him confidence.

Significant research proves how important journaling is for your health. An advanced psychiatric treatment study showed that journaling fifteen to twenty minutes for a minimum of only three to five days can show extraordinary results in helping you with dramatic events in your life. Additionally, a University of Iowa study showed that journaling provides conclusive assistance in helping you deal with all types of stress. That first twenty minutes writing in my journal on May 10, 2010 after my cancer diagnosis was huge and completely refocused my mindset.

> *Merely be quiet for fifteen minutes and just let your mind rest. Then began to write with no editing, no judgment, no other observations, just writing for yourself.*
>
> Michael Hyatt

This has proven to be one of the most stress-free activities you can do in the world. Thomas Jefferson, Charles Darwin, Ralph Waldo Emerson, Winston Churchill, and President Barack Obama are known for being vivacious journal writers. A wonderful site for setting up your journal can be found at www.dayoneapp.com. The following are some great activities that you can use to prepare yourself for any situation with your ruck.

Daily Activity Quotes
I love inspirational quotes. I keep a list of motivational quotes with me, and I start every day with daily positive affirmations from my

ruck. I carry three 3x5 cards with inspirational quotes every day. I have the following three quotes in my ruck beside me as I'm writing this on the plane from Stuttgart, Germany to Dublin, Ireland:

Seize the moment of happiness, love and be loved! That is the only one reality in the world.
Leo Tolstoy

Think of all the beauty still left around you and be happy.
Anne Frank

Happiness is a direction, not a place.
Sydney J. Harris

Read Every Day
The ability to look at different books at different times has drastically increased with the use of e-books. Sometimes you must sustain yourself for a while from your ruck and you don't have the ability to reach a Wi-Fi connection. Always have a few paperback books you can carry all the time in your ruck. I recommend you have books for spirit, inspiration, and enthusiasm.

My go-to softcover reading books in my ruck are:

1. *Unbroken* by Laura Hillenbrand
2. *Man's Search of Meaning* by Victor Frankl
3. *The Alchemist* by Paulo Coelho

Thank You Card Cache
Get a large Ziploc bag to protect your thank you cards from the elements. Create a thank you note cache that is easily accessible when you are ready to sit down and write one. Include nice card stock, stamps, and a variety of writing pens and note cards.

Passport and Identification
Secure your identification, and place it securely inside your ruck. Include the identification necessities such as passport, driver's license, and any other form of picture ID and required documents. Always place these items in a Ziploc bag to prevent them from getting wet. If you are traveling abroad, it's a good idea to make a copy of your passport and keep it somewhere else on your person. Also send a copy to a family member or friend. If you lose your passport, this makes the time at the embassy much easier.

Combination Lock and Change
It's just a good idea to carry the good old spin-dial Master Lock. In your travels, you may want to go to a fitness center or secure your bag in a locker somewhere else. The change is useful for public transportation, pay toilets, and pay lockers, and it is a good idea to get a small case for change.

The "B" Ruck Items

Virtual Ruck
Everything in your rucksack is not an actual physical presence. Some items in your rucksack are virtual or in the cloud. These items are at your disposal and usable at anytime. If I need something, for example, I can go to my notebook or my PDA, and I can pull these items up for immediate use.

Mentor
You can only mentor somebody if they want to be.

Phil Ramone

A mentor may be the most important item in your ruck, whether this is a tangible item or virtual. A mentor can serve as a counselor, a guide, a tutor, a guru, or an advisor. A mentor is somebody you can go to for advice any time.

Think for a moment about the last time you had an opportunity for promotion, a tragedy in your life, or experienced an upcoming change in your life or current job. Who would you call to share your news or ask advice? You should have a handful of people who you could call in various situations; however, you normally have one or two people who serve as a mentor.

We all end up with mentors from different aspects of our life. Professional athletes, schoolteachers, small business owners, family physicians, the bus driver, or the postman...anyone can be a mentor to others in their time of need. Anybody can give you good advice and set a good example for you to follow.

Feet Hit the Ground: The Three-Minute Rule
Virtually nothing is impossible in this world if you just put your mind to it and maintain a positive attitude.

Lou Holtz

I picked up this technique a long time ago in the military, and it's paid dividends ever since. My basic training instructor pulled me aside one day and said, "I'll give you a hint for success: Before your alarm goes off each morning, spend three minutes to say thanks for what you have—for your breath, your fulfilled life, your parents, your friends, your current opportunities." Then he told me, think about what you want to do today, and plan to do your best in every activity. Think about the people in your life: How will your accomplishments affect them? Think about the example you're setting to your family, your friends, your kids.

I perform this ritual every morning, before I start my day. I remind myself that *I'm relentless. I can do this. I am unstoppable. I am unbreakable.* Life is not intended to be easy. Between jobs, family issues, health issues, and launching new projects, this ritual and my mantra have stayed a constant in my life.

Every single morning.

Be Productive

Every day, all day I have to be productive. And when I ain't productive, I get concerned.

Young Jeezy

Take a look around you, and look how many people seem to be busy. Notice the busy activities outnumber the productive activities by a wide margin. You see busy people running all over the place, late to conferences, work, meetings, and social engagements. They hardly have enough time to do anything, really, and are usually lacking sleep and productivity.

The key to being productive is to slow down, review your commitments and goals, and put the first things first. Be proactive and do one thing at a time. Just being busy to look busy is a form of mental laziness and indiscriminate action. Learn to concentrate on the skill of working smarter, not harder.

My favorite line from my favorite Christmas movie, *Christmas Vacation* with Chevy Chase, is when the little girl tells the grandfather when the lights don't work on the house: "Daddy worked really hard on this house, Grandpa." Grandpa responds, "So do washing machines." You can have a lot of movement and be busy and still not be productive. Make it a point today to be productive.

Successful People Keep This Simple
The ability to simplify means to eliminate the unnecessary so that the necessary may speak.

Hans Hofmann

This is the beauty of the rucksack—simplicity. I've showed up multiple times in my life with everything I own in my ruck, and I was in paradise. Americans are becoming more like the rest of the world in adopting a minimalistic lifestyle, not carrying and packing a bunch of junk—which makes their life easier.

Leonardo da Vinci once said, "Simplicity is the ultimate sophistication." This is absolutely true. Use technology and information to your advantage. Technology can spin you out of control… or you can slow it down—you are in control. Turn off the cell, tablet, or computer and slow down the day a bit and keep it simple. We have choices when it comes to living our lives, our careers…but unfortunately this chaos creates complication and confusion. You need to simplify your life—the simpler, the better.

Try to Avoid Being Perfect
Strive for continuous improvement, instead of perfection.

Kim Collins

Many of us try to keep everything perfect all the time. What happens when we spend all of our time trying to be perfect? We become upset, down, and angry, and fail to meet the high standards that we set for ourselves. Perfectionists have a hard time finishing things, as they can never get a hundred-percent solution. Remember, the real world doesn't reward perfectionists. The world rewards people who get things done. I recommend reading *Overcoming Perfectionism: The Key to a Balanced Recovery* by Ann

W. Smith—an amazing read on conquering perfectionism for the "A" type people who must always be a hundred percent perfect all the time. Tyra Banks said it best: "I'm a perfectionist. Sometimes I have to remind myself that it's okay if there are flaws here and there."

Circle of Friends

True friendship is like sound health; the value of it is seldom known until it is lost.

Charles Caleb Colton

Did you know you're an average of your five closest friends? Look at your close circle of friends. What do you see? Chances are you see something that looks much like you.

Successful, energetic, and happy people associate themselves with the same type of supportive, like-minded, and focused people. This is why the military academies have such a successful reputation in continually producing successful leaders over such a long period of time. This tradition is attributed to a circle of friends who have the same values, discipline, and goals. Look at your five closest friends. Do they exemplify your characteristics, do they make you better? Or are they trying to get you to do things that are not positive for you? *Tribes* by Seth Godin is a fantastic read on this topic. It's actually very simple: associate yourself with positive, successful people who share your drive and goals. You attract what you think, you attract what you are, you attract what you hang around. If you hang around positivity—you will be a positive person.

Action

Step one

The Bob Hope "enjoying the moment" note: Over the next week, write one motivational note to yourself every day. End every note by writing, "I'm proud of myself, my success, and in the words of Les Brown, "I'm doing better than good and better than most!"

Step two

We have an entire section on the importance of giving thanks. However, I find it important to ensure that you have a reminder in your virtual rucksack to thank three people every day. I've received unbelievable responses from people all over the world—and better yet, I feel wonderful.

Sometimes I'm so busy that I find it difficult to stop in the middle of the day and find someone to thank. There have been times when I've found somebody to thank at the store, the market, or I've even gone to the street to find somebody—but every day I thank three people.

How many days in a row can you thank three people? You can thank them in person, e-mail, text, social media, or send a letter/postcard or make a phone call. Just thank them for being a friend, supportive, loyal or whatever the occasion. You will see a tremendous addition to your virtual rucksack.

Key Points

- Write in a journal daily to track your feelings, experiences, and mood
- Be productive, not busy
- Simplicity equals success
- Read for spirit, inspiration, and enthusiasm
- Use the three-minute rule every morning

ACTION

Chapter Eleven

Upgrade Your Personal Healthcare Plan

It was part of the reason I almost didn't go public with my diagnosis—
I was embarrassed. I felt, "Oh, I've always talked about exercising.
And I got cancer." And then I realized it's a great example
of showing that cancer can hit anyone at any time.

ROBIN ROBERTS

11

Take Full Responsibility for Your Health

The greatest day in your life and mine is when we take total responsibility for our attitudes. That's the day we truly grow up.

JOHN C. MAXWELL

This chapter is my personal experience from trying to live a healthy life…and then running into a major medical situation…and then rediscovering my health, my goals, and now beating the disease and living healthy.

You and only you are responsible for your own healthcare plan. I'm not talking about what type of insurance you have or where the hospital is located or how good the doctors are. This subject of personal healthcare is on you, and don't pawn this off on anyone else.

When we stop listening to our body, the problems begin. Eighty percent of hospital visits in America are related directly to stress. You must listen to your body and make sure that you're doing the things that you need to do to take care of yourself and decrease stress in your life.

This book has an abundance of information about understanding and listening to your body. A great start to a healthy body is facing stress head on with the following tools from this book:

- Journaling
- Yoga and Meditation
- Laughter
- Travel
- Friendship, Circle of Trust, and Strong Relationships
- Leveraging Positive Self-Talk
- Trust
- Use the Tools in Your Ruck
- One Hand on Your Duffel Bag
- Enthusiasm
- Finding that Happy Place
- Hunt the Good Stuff
- Giving Thanks

You have one body—treat it better than you do anything or anyone else in the world. Treat your body like you would your car...better yet, treat your body like you would an airplane and you're the pilot. To fly that airplane from point A to point B, you must ensure that aircraft is healthy. Do the same with your personal healthcare plan: Take full responsibility for everything that happens to you, and don't blame it on anybody else.

You must look at what you eat, how much you exercise, and what you're doing to relieve stress. Your journal is a great tool; write in your journal about your exercise, how different foods make you feel, and motivate yourself through your journal.

Just remember, everybody's personal situation is different. Get to know yourself and your situation.

No Excuses—Cancer Was My Fault

You must take personal responsibility. You cannot change the circumstances, the seasons, or the wind, but you can change yourself. That is something you have charge of.

Jim Rohn

When I look back and connect the dots up to my cancer diagnosis, I should have seen this coming. I've gone over thirty years working multiple jobs without a break. I thrived on deadlines and the need to be busy all the time.

I picked up this work ethic by watching how hard mother worked to raise my sister and me. Every time I've had an opportunity to work a second, third, and fourth job, I've always done so, remembering how hard my mother worked to raise us.

I've always looked at a job as an opportunity and not work. I've always been able to handle everything with complete enthusiasm—until my immune system broke down.

Slowing down was not in my nature. Like a car without a tune-up, I eventually hit the wall and medically needed to go to the garage for maintenance. Between commuting, training, creating, working, and planning, I never allowed my body the opportunity to rest and become silent. I just continued to push, push, push—until May 10, 2010...and that's when my body said, *That's enough!* Although I was healthy on the outside, I was not handling the stress properly on the inside...to the garage I go!

Cancer Diagnosis

You hear the word "cancer," and you think it is a death sentence. In fact, the shock is the biggest thing about a diagnosis of cancer.

Clare Balding

In late January 2010, I developed a sore throat but not a fever, so I waited five days before I went to my first medical appointment to get antibiotics. Something felt very odd about the sore throat without the normal symptoms of the flu or strep throat. These symptoms continued for the next two months as I traveled with my team around the world, visiting various emergency rooms, medical clinics, and hospitals every five to seven days with the continued symptom of a sore throat.

I served as a medical service corps officer for sixteen years in the United States Army and witnessed some of the best healthcare in the world—I'm talking absolute state-of-the-art, cutting-edge medical equipment and dedicated healthcare providers who work everywhere from combat medicine to large fixed medical centers.

During my travels around the world from mid-January to late March, I was seen thirteen different times in both military and civilian medical treatment facilities. During this process, I was diagnosed with strep throat twice without ever receiving a throat culture or the doctor looking into my throat. I was given Motrin twice for pain, and two other times the healthcare provider looked down my throat, yet didn't see anything, even with the tongue depressor (although less than a month later, it took only a glance by the ENT doctor with a tongue depressor to see the tumor that was bulging inside my throat).

I'm just as guilty as anybody in this process. I'm an optimist, always looking at the glass half-full and saying to myself, *I'm okay,*

I've always been healthy, and eventually this will go away. I was doing what many men do: not raising the red flag when I knew my body was not normal. As long as the physician's assistant or nurse said I was okay, I was fine with that.

I continued to travel and work, pacified by what different doctors had told me. I finally said enough is enough, realizing I had been in denial long enough. I made an appointment in April 2010 with my healthcare provider. As my sore throat had persisted for three months, I asked to see an ear, nose, and throat specialist. I was given an appointment with an ENT specialist for June—two months away! Despite this, I did not raise the issue any more now that I had an actual appointment to see a specialist.

The following day we departed for our next trip to Tulsa, Oklahoma. That evening in Oklahoma, I started coughing up blood from my throat and base of my tongue area. I contacted the hospital; they insisted on bringing me in to do x-rays of my lungs. I tried to explain that the pain has been coming from my throat, that I'd been losing weight and energy, and that I wasn't coughing anything from my lungs. An appointment was made a couple days later to have my lungs x-rayed. Everything was clear, and I was given the go-ahead to return to work, but the problem persisted: I continued to cough up blood, though it was getting thicker and more frequent. I was finally scheduled to see an ENT on May 7, 2010, three months after the start of my sore throat. Three months later, and I was finally going to a specialist.

The ENT saw the tumor right away. Seven centimeters in size. "We need to do a biopsy right away," he said. I asked him what he thought the prognosis was. He removed his glasses and sighed, looked at me, and said, "I just don't want to speculate at this point. Let's wait until the biopsy results come in on Monday."

You know how you get the feeling that something is not quite right? A small part of me knew that I could be as positive as I wanted, but this was going to be a much bigger issue. I knew that my Monday biopsy would change my life.

In keeping with my optimistic, enthusiastic attitude, I decided to give myself a present, no matter the outcome on Monday. I've always had a strong desire to get back to Germany and dreamed of buying a Mercedes-Benz sedan.

Since my future could very well be left in the balance on Monday, I decided to go to the Mercedes dealer in Kansas City and pick one out. I bought that beautiful used C230 Mercedes on Friday and took it home on Saturday. I promised myself to keep the car locked in my garage until after the biopsy when I was cleared medically from this situation.

The biopsy was complete on May 10, 2010, and it was confirmed that I had squamous cell cancer stage III at the base of my tongue. The cancer had manifested itself in a very large tumor. The next chapter of my life was about to begin. That Mercedes would stay in my garage until I completed the treatment. The Mercedes was my visualization and my gift to myself for when we were finished with wherever this diagnosis would take me.

I visualized driving that car down the highway cancer-free.

I take full responsibility for waiting so long to raise the issue of my sore throat when I realized how serious it was becoming after one month. I simply fell into the trap that it couldn't be anything serious and that it would get better. "Not me; nothing bad could ever happen to me," right?

From the time I entered the military at eighteen, I've received nothing but amazing healthcare. My entire medical team conveyed the same message before my treatment started. They each told me that I had a distinct advantage over everybody else because I had military medicine in my personal file. I went into that fight an extremely healthy person because of the healthcare I'd received since I was a teenager.

I accept personal responsibility for the time it took in determining a diagnosis. I let the cancer take over my body when I knew something was wrong. The diagnosis had been made, and I decided I would get myself out of this situation, and I was determined to be cancer-free.

The Standard in Cancer Care: The University of Kansas Cancer Center

I believe the greatest gift you can give your family and the world is a healthy you.

Joyce Meyer

My healthcare at the University of Kansas Cancer Center was nothing short of amazing. One by one, in my initial meetings with each of my providers (Dr. Shnayder, Dr. Kumar, Dr. Neupani, and Dr. Lausten), they would close the door, sit me down, and look me eye to eye to tell me, "You can make this, you will beat this, we have the best cancer facility in the world, and with your attitude, this cancer does not stand a chance."

As a professional communicator and a longtime teacher in interpersonal communication, I cannot tell you how much it meant that each of the four doctors, who had my life in their hands, took time to look me in the eye and tell me, "You're going to be okay."

My entire cancer team was under one roof, and I did not have to run to several different facilities for different checkups. All of my treatment and healthcare providers were done together—my team of surgeons, radiologists, chemo docs, oncology dentists, nutritionists, and depression or psychology assistance personnel worked together under one roof, making the treatment seamless and effective.

This book is about motivation, enthusiasm, overcoming great adversity, strength, and achieving your goals and dreams. The day I first met my medical team, I tried to show strength on the outside with smiles, laughter, and even delivering my first initial set of thank you notes. However...

I was terrified.

I remember shaking so bad I could not get my finger to push the button on the elevator to go up to the floor for my first checkup. The short consultation I spent with each doctor on my team made the difference between me starting my cancer treatment at a standstill or with a hundred percent momentum. The confidence of my medical team allowed me to completely put all Three Points of Contact to work.

As I write this book four years after my initial cancer diagnosis, the doctors, nurses, healthcare technicians, and everybody at the University of Kansas Cancer Center are like family, and they will be for life. To the entire staff at the University of Kansas Cancer Center, I am alive today in large part because of you!

Thank you for your love, your care, and your enduring professionalism during my treatment. Carpe diem! I encourage anyone to contact me if you have any questions about the recommendation and the care I received.

**It's my honor to donate a portion of the proceeds for the life of this book to the University of Kansas Cancer Center Department of Radiation Oncology, Otolaryngology and the Support for People with Oral and Head and Neck Cancer (SPOHNC).

Just Start Moving—Find Your Activity and Get Back in the Game!

The more you frame the marathon as a stressful experience, the more negative messages you'll receive. But it's just as easy to frame it as a positively challenging journey.

Jeff Galloway

The first thing you want to do when you finish something like cancer treatment, illness, or any setback is to start physical exercise and get active. Begin physical activity and push yourself—push yourself to your limit. I wanted to feel as normal as possible and competitive again.

I set a goal to run a marathon during the beginning of treatment—therefore, the logical thing for me to do was start training properly for the marathon. I read a marathon-training guide by Jeff Galloway and subscribed to a podcast named the Marathon Training Academy (MTA). I sent Mr. Galloway a message on Facebook and didn't anticipate a response, as he's one of the most popular running coaches in the world. Mr. Galloway returned my request and gave me some amazing advice. MTA has a personal coaching plan you can subscribe to for a small fee. The MTA comes with personal interaction from the wife/husband team of Angie and Trevor. The combined run/walk instruction by Jeff and the personal training from MTA were invaluable.

I'm still using the advice from all three as I've run four half-marathons and eight full marathons. I'm training for my ninth marathon in New York in November 2015. Thanks, Jeff and the MTA team!

Walk Your Way to Amazing Health!

*My grandmother started walking five miles a day when she
was sixty. She's ninety-seven now, and we don't know where
the hell she is.*

Ellen DeGeneres

The New England Journal of Medicine recently reported on
the twelve-year Honolulu Heart Study of 8,000 men. The study
was conducted by the Kuakini Honolulu Heart Program (HHP)
on the island of Oahu.

The study reports that walking just two miles a day cuts the
risk of death almost in half. The walkers' risk of death was especially lower for cancer.

Walking is a great activity and is one of the easiest ways to
increase your physical activity and improve your health. Regular
walking has been shown to reduce the risk of chronic illnesses,
such as heart disease, type 2 diabetes, asthma, stroke, and many
cancers.

*Longer, moderately-paced daily walks are best for
losing weight.*

*Shorter, faster walks are best for conditioning your
heart and lungs.*

Being consistent in your walking exercise routine is one of the
most important factors in developing a healthy physical activity
program. Research has shown that people who walk approximately
twenty to twenty-five miles per week outlive those who don't walk
by several years. You improve your chances of protecting the heart

and circulatory system by raising HDL, the good cholesterol, and keeping weight down.

Make Walking a Habit—
Just Like in Europe

A vigorous five-mile walk will do more good for an unhappy but otherwise healthy adult than all the medicine and psychology in the world.

Paul Dudley White

I started walking with a pedometer to monitor my goals during my cancer treatment, and I've walked ever since. Europe's walking culture is a main reason why I wanted to come to Germany as soon as possible. The healthy outdoor lifestyle of Europe is what I wanted—that was my "happy place."

I visualized riding the bus/train/streetcar to and from work every day. Getting on the train to Paris, Munich, Salzburg, Zurich, London, just to name a few cities, and walking all over Europe.

I'm alive today because I walk from the time I get up in the morning until I go to sleep at night. I walk amidst eleventh-century buildings, amazing culture, and the healthy and lively people everywhere. Walking is fitness, meditation, circulatory, and it cleanses my mind.

My daily preventative medicine is walking 20,000 steps.

Europe is a walking culture. The quote below explains why Europeans are extremely fit. I've lived in Stuttgart, Germany for almost four years—everybody walks everywhere. This is the home of Mercedes, Porsche, and BMW, but the fitness of the citizens comes from walking.

*Research reveals that walking just an extra twenty
minutes each day
will burn off seven pounds of body fat per year!*

Europeans take public transportation everywhere—not a lot of
sitting in front of the television and driving cars to work over here!
Research shows that for every hour of brisk walking, life expec-
tancy for some people may increase by up to two hours or more.
Henry David Thoreau stated:

An early-morning walk is a blessing for the whole day.

The easiest way to walk more is to take action and make walking a habit. Think of ways to include walking into your daily routine. Examples include:

- Walk part of your journey to work.
- Park farther away in the parking lot.
- Use the stairs instead of the elevator.
- Use public transportation as often as you can.
- Go for a walk after every meal.

Set Yourself a Goal

*Stay focused, go after your dreams, and keep moving toward
your goals.*

LL Cool J

Act now, and make walking a habit. Treat walking exercise
just like brushing your teeth. Once you've made walking a habit,
set a longer-term goal. You may begin by setting a goal for walking

briskly for at least thirty minutes a day or start with 1,000 steps a day and work up to 10,000 steps a day. The sky's the limit! Watch your overall health and outlook on life flourish.

Mineral Water, Natural Water, and Cut out the Sodas

Drinking water is like washing out your insides. The water will cleanse the system, fill you up, decrease your caloric load and improve the function of all your tissues.

Kevin R. Stone

Drinking mineral water diminished my desire to drink sodas completely. Mineral water is easy to find in Germany, as they have literally hundreds of mineral water preferences. When I'm back in the States, my favorite is Gerolsteiner, Perrier, Pellegrino, or another brand of mineral water (or, if nothing else, soda water will work).

I have a carafe I use for natural water, and I can simply add strawberries, blueberries, lemon, or lime, and it seems to do very well for me. I enjoy it, it's refreshing, and it helps with my throat. Yes, even after four and a half years, my throat is still a little dry with my diminished saliva glands from the radiation. Water works wonders.

Many of my clients have a difficult time cutting back or quitting sodas altogether. Here's a tip to get off the carbonated sodas: Take a Ziploc bag and fill the bag with the amount of sugar you consume in daily soft drinks. The average is two tablespoons for each twelve-ounce can...not to mention all the other preservatives, but that is a conversation for another day. Carry that bag of sugar with you everywhere until you stop drinking the sodas. Many people don't recognize the large amount of sugar they consume until they see it right in front of them.

Juicing

After doing a juice cleanse, I'm motivated to eat healthier and not emotionally. Cleansing is like my meditation. It makes me stop, focus, and think about what I'm putting into my body. I'm making a commitment.

Salma Hayek

I recommend this nutrition activity for everyone. I picked this up as supplemental nutrition during my radiation and cancer treatment. I mixed fruits, vegetables, and protein in my juicer and put it directly in my stomach tube.

Amazing how much better I feel when I juice! Juicing has been a key to keeping my weight down with the loss of my thyroid from the radiation. There are many good juicing products; I recommend the Vitamix, as it's strong, sturdy, and easy to clean and maintain. I use the Vitamix for juice, salsa, and soups, and I juice to support my daily fitness regimen and meal plan. I will occasionally do a reboot cleanse and just juice for twenty-four to forty-eight hours. My body feels completely energized after every short reboot.

My Thyroid Is Gone...And I Feel Great!

The greatest wealth is health.

Virgil

Something interesting happened after I ran my first half-marathon in Munich after I arrived in Germany in 2011. I was just over one year cancer-free, and complete with a regimen of exercise, eating healthy, drinking great mineral water, and living the outdoor lifestyle of Europe, I felt fantastic. Suddenly I gained thirty pounds in one month. My thyroid finally lost any functionality due to the radiation treatment.

Don't let anybody tell you that because you have a thyroid problem, you're going to have a major weight problem. This is not true; you just need to adjust your exercise, your diet, the time you eat, and everything about your well-being to support the change in your body (read the chapter Turn It All Off). For me, the big change was the time I could eat, the time for fitness, what I could eat, and proper medication. I go to the clinic every six months to get my blood checked, my metabolism checked, blood pressure checked, and to see a nutritionist if I need to change or adjust my food plan. I feel better and stronger and healthier than I did twenty-five years ago.

Go see your physician to get started in the right direction. Become a student and expert of your particular medical situation. Don't allow anything or anyone else to advise you on your medical situation. Stand up straight and with your physician's direction and the lessons from the Three Points of Contact—you've got this! Feel free to contact me if you need some motivational encouragement.

Action

Get back in the game

This activity is about getting you back into the game. Let's call the first step a snowflake. Sign up for an activity and attend for one week. The snowflake is going to build momentum, and you will continue to go forward or you will find another activity—creating a small snowball. This activity will turn into energy and enthusiasm. The activity could be running a 5K, biking to work, walking a certain number of pedometer steps a day, getting up from work every hour and going for a walk, skipping the big lunch with colleagues and doing some exercise, deciding not to watch TV for a week and instead doing some activity, or going to the gym. Get back out with the public, and get back in the game. Before you know it, your snowball will be growing, tumbling down the hill, and you'll be in a healthy fitness regimen.

Let me know what activity you did today! I'd like to hear where you're at today, a week from now, a month of now, a year from now, and beyond on that activity. Good luck, and get back in the game!

Tune-up time

This is time for your healthcare tune-up. Brainstorm all of your goals, obstacles, roadblocks, and people you need to contact. Take ten minutes and brainstorm all the medical requirements you have during any given year. Dental, semiannual checkups, flu shots, glasses/optometry, nutrition, fitness, yoga/stillness/meditation, and other checkups that are required based on your medical background.

Take a piece of paper and draw line down the middle. Draw a plus (+) in the top left and a minus (-) in the top right. In the left column, add all the different healthcare areas you have met in the past year. In the right column, write down what you didn't get a chance to do, as well as personal healthcare areas you want to do but you have not done—maybe a massage, yoga, playing golf, tennis, jogging, attending a Zumba class, or swimming.

Look at your list and take the items in the (+) column and place them in your calendar for the next twelve months. In the (-) column, begin this week and place those items on your calendar. If you need to make a massage, pedicure, or cardio class appointment, go ahead and do so. You will see a drastic change in your healthcare plan as you place these items on your calendar. Send me a note; I'd love to hear how you're doing.

Key Points

Always listen to your body—it will tell you when something is wrong

Become passionate about an activity and do it daily

Make healthy changes—walking, mineral water, and juicing

Laughter, trust, and travel are just a few things that improve your well-being

ACTION

Chapter Twelve

Communicate Like Your Life Depends on It!

*Communication—the human connection—is the
key to personal and career success.*

PAUL J. MEYER

12

A Skill You MUST Conquer

Number one, cash is king... number two, communicate.

JACK WELCH

Communication is the number one human characteristic that leads to success.

It was only natural that one of my 12.5 methods would be focused on the art of effective communication. I've spent the better part of my life studying how people communicate with each other. I'm fascinated by how the ability to communicate can make the difference between average and extremely successful. I noticed this when I caddied as a teenager. I listened to the golfers interact and immediately knew who were the attorneys, businessmen, doctors, and leading educators by the way they communicated. As a young airman, I saw how the effective communicators moved up the ladder. Communication and being a leader in the armed forces is synonymous to leading soldiers anywhere.

This chapter is about you becoming a confident communicator. The focus is the art of verbal and non-verbal communicative skills as you prepare for success before, during, and after any storm. The chapter consists of listening and speaking skills. Know the key to victory is to communicate.

Leverage Your Listening Skills

It is not the voice that commands the story; it is the ear.
Italo Calvino

Listening builds trust between yourself and the speaker. Most colleges offer a communication class or two for any major. However, you can Google *listening, CEO, business,* and *executive skills* and you will see communication skills and listening ranked on every chart. Listening is not automatic—it takes hard work, continuous practice, and is an extremely valuable skill. Learn to be an active listener. Active listeners lean forward and are actively involved in the conversation. Work on the following activities and put yourself completely ahead of the competition. Remember, nobody likes a lazy listener—get out there and set the example!

Face the Speaker and Focus on Eye Contact

Nothing is more distracting than trying to talk to people while they are scanning the room, gazing out the window, or appear to be inattentive. How much actual attention are you giving the speaker? Ten percent? Fifty percent? Maybe none at all? Have the courtesy to turn and face the speaker while he or she is speaking. Put aside papers, books, electronic media, and other distractions. Look at the speaker even if he or she doesn't look at you. Shyness, guilt, shame, and uncertainty can inhibit eye contact in some people. You are not that person! Show respect and stay focused on the speaker.

A tip that I use while listening to a speaker and concentrate on maintaining eye contact: I grab my journal and take notes to stay focused and attentive. This gives the speaker complete assurance that you are focusing on him or her. Put a motivational note in your journal to remind yourself to stay focused, maintain eye contact, and smile. This journal note will allow you the chance to refocus.

Listen to the Words and Try to Picture What the Speaker is Saying

Create a mental picture of the information being communicated, even if it's a literal picture or an abstract concept. Your brain will connect the dots and create a clear message. Focus with all your senses and remain fully alert. When you are listening for long periods of time, concentrate and remember keywords and phrases and write them down in your journal.

When it's your turn to listen, don't spend your thought process time figuring out what to say next. Think only about what the person is saying in the present moment. If your thoughts begin to wander because of lack of interest in the topic, you must refocus again. Listening is hard work but is critical in you getting that interview, job, promotion, and advancement in life. Be active!

Remain Open-Minded

Listen without judging the other speaker or criticizing. As soon as you start judging the communicative message, you degrade your effectiveness as a listener. Listen without jumping to conclusions. Remember that the speaker is using language to represent the thoughts and feelings inside of his or her brain. You don't know what those thoughts and feelings are, and you will not be able to understand until you are able to listen with a full mind. The journal is a great tool to ensure your mind stays open. It's unrealistic to think that you're going to listen to a message a hundred percent of the time. You are capable of understanding speech up to 700 to 800 words per minute; however, the average person speaks only 140 to 160 words per minute. If something else pops into your mind, write it down in your journal, and immediately get back and start listening with an open mind.

Wait to Ask Questions

Wait for the speaker to pause or finish before you ask any questions. When you don't understand something, you should ask the speaker to explain it to you. Don't interrupt in the middle of a discussion or presentation. Wait until the speaker pauses or finishes and is ready to answer questions. To avoid interrupting, wait three seconds before you reply to the speaker. This pause will help build your rapport, as it gives a strong indication that you are giving thought and are interested in what the speaker is saying.

Don't Interrupt and Don't Impose

Be patient and listen.

Interrupting sends a variety of messages to the speaker to include—most notably, that your opinion is more important than the speaker's. This really becomes the case in one-on-one interactions. We all think and speak at a different tone and rate, and everyone has a different speed in which to speak and think. You must relax and be a thoughtful listener as well as a communicator.

When listening to someone talk about a problem, avoid making suggestions in the middle of the presentation. If you have an amazing idea that you must suggest, please ask the speaker, "I have an idea—would you like to hear it?" This really is a top rule in courtesy listening one-on-one and in group settings. Again, be patient and listen.

Avoid "Stage Hogging"

You're at work, and a colleague is telling you about a wonderful trip she had to the Sierra Nevadas and all the wonderful things she did and saw. In the course of the story, she mentioned that she spent some time with a mutual friend. You jump in: "Oh, I haven't heard from this mutual friend in ages. How is she?" And just like that, the discussion shifts to this other person, and to divorce, kids, needing to change schools, and on and on. Before you know it, an hour has passed, and the conversation about the Sierra Nevadas is long gone.

This particular stage hogging happens daily. Our questions lead people in directions that have nothing to do with where they were going with the story. Sometimes we get back to the original story, but very often we don't. If you notice that your question has taken the speaker away from the original story, take responsibility for getting the conversation back on track by saying something like, "It's great to hear about our friend, but please go back and tell me about the Sierra Nevadas."

How many times does this happen to you over the course of the day? Some of us have friends that do this all the time—and it's one of the most irritating things to deal with when you're trying to get a message across.

Relax and Pay Attention

You can relax now that you've made eye contact. You don't have to stay transfixed and stare at the speaker. In one-on-one conversations, it's okay to look away now and then and carry on normal conversation. Pay attention—and this means apply yourself, give attention, be present, and look genuinely interested in the speaker and topic. Again, use a journal or notebook to write in—it's always a good technique. Block out any distractions such as background activity and noise. Try not to focus on any of the speaker's mannerisms to the point where they become distractions. Don't allow your thoughts, biases, and feelings to get in the way of concentrating on the speaker's message.

Put Yourself in the Speaker's Place

Empathy is the center point of good listening.

You express sadness when the person who is talking expresses sadness, joy when the person is happy, fear when the person expresses fear. You are now an effective listener when you convey these feelings with facial expressions and words. Empathy is expressed when you allow yourself to put yourself in the speaker's shoes and see what it feels like to be him or her for a moment. This is a difficult thing to do, as it takes incredible energy and concentration. Genuine and heartfelt empathy is an art and a skill.

Practice and learn it!

Feedback Is Showing that You Care

Show you understand what the speaker is talking about by reflect-ing the speaker's feelings. The easiest way is to do this is with a simple nod, a smile, or by showing active attentiveness. Be active and attentive.

Public Speaking for Success

The single biggest problem in communication is the illusion that it has taken place.

George Bernard Shaw

The ability to communicate powerfully and prolifically was ranked as one of the top skills for a leader's success in article in the Harvard Business Review. Effective communication is an in-valuable asset you will use every day of your life. Studies show that effective communication improves success in your education, interview skills, communicating with colleagues, communicating with supervisors, networking, giving presentations, and commu-nication is involved in our everyday life. Your opportunities for a successful, fulfilled, and happy life are centered on your ability to communicate.

The following section will focus on key tips for public speak-ing and giving short presentations. The information for this sec-tion will be based on research, and listening to, evaluating, and grading over 5,000 presentations, those from college students and from clients around the world. Focus on these tips, and you will be on your way to an effective, successful presentation experience.

Rehearse, Rehearse, Rehearse!

The audience knows in the first thirty seconds whether your presentation is rehearsed or not. Nothing replaces proper rehearsal. If you don't rehearse and are unprepared, the audience will turn you off.

Try to rehearse in front of somebody who can give you actual feedback. Making a visual recording of your presentation is another effective way of rehearsal. No matter how you get around it, you cannot avoid rehearsing for your presentation—this is key and a requirement for successful presentations!

Stage Fright, Communication Apprehension, and Plain Nervousness

In a recent Gallup poll, Americans were asked to list their greatest fears. Forty percent identified speaking before a group as a top fear, exceeded only by fifty-one percent who said they were afraid of snakes. In comparison, only twenty-eight percent said they were afraid of dying. In most polls, speechmaking and speaking in front of a group of people is tops in provoking anxiety (stage fright). If you are nervous or suffer tremendous anxiety before giving a presentation, you have company including Abraham Lincoln, Margaret Sanger, Winston Churchill, Oprah Winfrey, Conan O'Brien, and Jay Leno. In his early career, Leonardo DiCaprio was so nervous about giving an acceptance speech that he hoped he would not win the award. Comedian Jerry Seinfeld said in jest (but sometimes it seems literally true), "Given a choice, at a funeral most of us would rather be the one in the coffin to the one giving the eulogy."

Nervousness about speaking is natural and is actually good for your speech delivery process. Anxiety helps you with nervous energy, and it will subside once the presentation begins. However, I allude to the first part of this section—nothing can replace rehearsal, rehearsal, rehearsal! We can discuss relaxation, affirmations, listening to music, or even doing yoga.

But there's nothing that replaces rehearsal for a presentation.

Extemporaneous Speaking

There is nothing worse than somebody delivering a presentation and reading from the manuscript word for word. How many of you have attended a presentation or required training and the presenter is reading word for word from the visual slides? This is wasting my time, the audience's time, and quite honestly will just bore you to tears. Reading the manuscript word for word eliminates effective eye contact, vocal variety, or tone and rate fluctuation. We've all seen the presentation where the presenter reads two or three lines and then glances at the audience, only to look back down to read two or three more lines and glance back to the audience. This is brutal!

Extemporaneous speaking is delivering your presentation away from your manuscript. This method requires you to know the content of your speech extremely well. In fact, when you use this method properly, you become so familiar with the substance of your talk that you need only a few brief notes to remind you of the key points you intend to present.

Your notes should consist of just a few keywords, phrases, or key points, rather than complete sentences and paragraphs. When you speak extemporaneously, this allows you to maintain complete eye contact with the audience, establish a variance in tone and rate, and provide your own personal style and delivery. Reading word for word or even memorizing the manuscript takes away all of your personal speaking characteristics.

Highlight keywords, terms, and phrases. Take those key terms and phrases and put them on note cards. Pull the note card out, and you can extemporaneously speak to the audience on the topic. This takes practice, but it's so enjoyable to do—and your speeches will be successful.

The Two-Minute Outline

This simple two-minute speaking outline will put you on the way of being in the top one percent of all speakers.

You will be in the top one percent of delivering any informative, demonstrative, or impromptu presentation by mastering this two-minute outline. The outline for the impromptu presentation will work for your demonstration and most other presentations. Obviously, in an impromptu presentation you do not have time to write out a full sentence manuscript. The following is the two-minute outline to provide you success for any presentation.

Every presentation has three parts: introduction, body, and conclusion. In essence, tell the audience what you want to tell them, tell them again what you said you were going to tell them, and tell them again what you told them you were going to tell them in the beginning.

I speak to everyone in the same way, whether he is the garbage man or the president of the university.

Albert Einstein

Introduction (Topic)
Attention-getter: Grab the audience's attention. Use a rhetorical question, quotation, startling statement, analogy, or short story.

Reason to listen: Give the audience the reason to listen to this topic.

Speaker credibility: Your credibility to speak in this topic.

Signposting: Preview and state the main points (keep between three and five main points).

The body

Three to five main points: Try to use personal experiences, five W's (who, what, when, where, and why). If you have short preparation time, these make it easy-to-recall information and speak extemporaneously.

Transition from point to point: Take the audience from main point to main point.

Conclusion

Restatement of the main points: Restate the signposting.

Tie this comment back to your attention-getter: Simply make a statement that takes the audience back to the attention-getter.

Reason to remember: This should leave the audience wanting more. Give the audience a quote or reason to remember this presentation.

Fill in the pieces, rehearse, highlight, place the bulleted comments on 3x5 cards, and you're ready to go. You now have a structured format for a presentation that you can use for any type of presentation. You are now in the top one percent of the thousands of students and clients I've worked with. Congratulations...now start speaking!

Eye Contact

The eyes have been called the windows of the soul.

They gauge the speaker's truthfulness, intelligence, attitudes, and feelings. The quickest way to establish a connection with your listeners is to look at them directly, while one of the quickest ways to lose your audience is to avoid eye contact.

Speakers who fail to establish eye contact are perceived as tentative or ill-at-ease and may be seen as disingenuous or insincere. It isn't enough just to look at your listeners; how you look at them also counts. When addressing a small audience, you can usually look briefly from person to person and make eye contact for three to five seconds each. For larger audience rooms, you can scan the audience, rather than lock-in with each person individually.

No matter the size of the audience, you want your eyes to portray confidence, sincerity, and conviction. Eye contact will improve with confidence, and confidence only comes from practice.

Speak with Passion

Memorable presentations are delivered with passion, energy, and enthusiasm.

The old saying is if something is worth doing, it's worth doing right. If the presentation is worth doing, it's worth doing with passion. You cannot have a passionate presentation that is read from the manuscript. The presentation must be performed with an extemporaneous delivery. Extemporaneous delivery allows the speaker to engage the audience with direct eye contact and fluctuating tone, rate, and vocal variety. Don't forget to smile. When you smile, you ease the audience, and it will ease yourself as well.

Rehearse, Rehearse, Rehearse!

Back where we started—remember to practice until you think you are ready. When you are ready, give your all, have fun, smile, and be enthusiastic.

Action

The talking stick

Have you ever been a part of a meeting where all the participants are talking at the same time? Everyone is so busy giving his or her opinion that nobody is listening to what is going on.

The talking stick reminds us that before we lead, we must listen. Leaders seek to understand the perspectives of others before they communicate their own points. The talking stick exercises the known fact that talking is easier than listening. This exercise is based on the Native American tradition of counsel.

Gather a group in a circle, and designate a particular object as the talking stick (almost any large object will do). Only the person holding the talking stick may speak. After each member the group has had a chance to speak, discuss your experiences. You'll be amazed what it's like when you realize the skill of listening to others speak.

Communicate without looking

Body language and eye contact are the two most important aspects of effective communication. This activity has eliminated these two aspects.

Sit back-to-back with your partner and converse about any given topic. After the conversation ends, see how this conversation, devoid of any eye contact, was different from a normal conversation. The main aim behind this activity is to explain the importance of eye contact and body language for effective communication.

Key Points

- Communication is the most important trait to foster relationships and well-being
- Maintain eye contact and listen
- Nervous energy for public speaking can be a good thing!
- Speak clearly and follow an outline
- Speak with passion about your subject
-

12. 5

Live Every Day with Enthusiasm

1 2. 5

Live Every Day with Enthusiasm

Just like the well-crafted hand written thank you note,
enthusiasm sets you apart from everybody else.

13

Enjoy Now—Live in the Moment

Be here now. Be someplace else later. Is that so complicated?

DAVID BADER

Enthusiastic people live today!

You cannot be enthusiastic if you become completely engaged in what happened yesterday or what's going to happen tomorrow. Focus your will and strength on living today. Don't worry about what happened yesterday, last year, or what's is in store for you in the future.

So many people cannot enjoy life with enthusiasm and passion because they are so worried about connecting the dots to the future for something they cannot see. It's difficult to live with enthusiasm and be proactive and passionate about life if you're waiting to see the dots line up before you.

The world is full of unhappy people who wake up every day and go to a job that they don't like—because that's the current dot, and they are waiting to be told to step on the next dot.

Get enthusiastic and take a chance…live!

The question is not whether there is life after death, the question is did you live while you were alive?

Osho

Enthusiastic People Live with Passion and Purpose

Enthusiasm is everything. It must be taut and vibrating like a guitar string.

Pele

Enthusiastic people have two purposes in life: a specific purpose and a pictorial purpose.

1. *Specific purpose* engages you and drives you to be enthusiastic. This is also known as the purpose of happiness. You will unquestionably know when you are there. You will feel ultimate happiness, joy, energy, and passion. You always want to be proactive and engaged. I'm in purposeful happiness when I teach a community college class, speak to an audience, write this book, speak to a sports team, work with inner-city youth, run, spend time with my children, and do practically anything that has to do with communication—that is my flow, Zen, bliss, and ultimate purpose of happiness. My yoga definitely puts me into a specific purpose. I'm completely refreshed and jazzed after each yoga session.

2. *Pictorial purpose* is linking a vivid picture to your goal or dream. I've had a pictorial purpose for all successful goals obtained. Whether I obtain the picture, draw a picture, or carry a memento, I have a visual pictorial purpose that I can see.

a   Arnold Schwarzenegger's pictorial purpose was a *Muscle and Fitness* magazine picture of Reg Park he saw as a teenager. Arnold visualized being a bodybuilder and an actor like Reg Park.

b   Taylor Swift watched a *Behind the Music* episode about Faith Hill and decided at age eleven she needed to go to Nashville. Taylor followed her pictorial purpose all the way to stardom.

This is the vision of the three points—that you can see it, taste it, smell it so bad that you will not stop until you're done. You maintain this enthusiasm with a combination of passion and purpose through opportunities.

Nobody is going to create your opportunity for you.

People want to be around enthusiastic, energetic, and passionate people.

Mary Marcdante, the author of *The Six Characteristics of Enthusiastic People*, exclaims that the number one characteristic of enthusiastic people is their ability to radiate positive energy. When these people walk into a room, heads turn and people gather. To embody this characteristic, you must dare to be different! Life is great; get excited about it. Go out and enjoy it and live with passion.

Dreams

There is real magic in enthusiasm. It spells the difference between mediocrity and accomplishment.

Norman Vincent Peale

Enthusiastic, passionate, and opportunistic people have dreams. Enthusiastic people always have something to look forward to and a dream for the future. Your dream might be purchasing a house on the ocean, traveling the world, learning how to do some type of recreational sport, establishing a charitable foundation, or teaching secondary school. Dreamful, enthusiastic people are goal-minded people. When you achieve goals (no matter how small or big), these milestones build momentum into a snowball effect and give you motivation. The snowball will get bigger and bigger as it rolls downhill. Ever felt like you were trying to get motivated and going uphill? Trying to lose weight, going back to school, learning a new language? Just do a little at a time and you will build momentum. Set small daily goals of action and you will be amazed at the progress.

When your enthusiasm doesn't go so well and you lose your enthusiastic "Mojo, baby," what would Austin Powers do? Get back out there and get small accomplishments in your court, and put it all in your journal and build that momentum.

What about the daily enthusiasm *dream killers*? You know the people who don't like seeing you enthusiastic, passionate, happy, and are always shooting down your ideas, thoughts, and aspirations? Disregard the enthusiasm killers and continue to move forward.

Winston Churchill stated, "Success consists of going from failure to failure without losing enthusiasm."

In life, you are either in a problem, leaving a problem, or entering a new problem and, simultaneously, you must maintain your enthusiasm at all times. Your ability to maintain your enthusiasm by focusing on your specific purpose, then picturing and actually seeing this purpose in your mind and living every day with passion will be a key to your success. Remember to use your Bulletin Board Material (BBM) as a driving force.

Forgive and Wish Them Well

Forgiveness is a perfectly selfish act. It sets you free from the past.
                                                      Brian Tracy

The quote above is solely about setting yourself free so you can move on and live your life with one hundred percent enthusiasm. In order for you to be entirely enthusiastic, you must forgive, forget, and wish them well. You will not get ahead holding grudges and holding onto something that happened in the past.

Randy Pausch, author of *The Last Lecture*, stated, "Brick walls are not there to keep us apart. They are there to give us a chance to show how badly we want something." You must be proactive to break down that forgiveness brick wall. Jump over that wall, fix this situation immediately, and set yourself free. Free yourself so you can move on with a life of total belief and passion.

If you continue to hold grudges, resentment, and hard feelings, you will not be able to move forward. You will be caught in the same trap you were in trying to connect the dots to the future.

If you need to apologize or forgive somebody, now's the time to do it. You must release your inner self in order to be enthusiastic every single day. The road to ultimate enthusiasm begins with ultimate and sincere forgiveness.

Brian Tracy recommends that you MUST forgive the following four people in your life. Forgive and set yourself free, and enjoy a life of ultimate joy and enthusiasm. Let's look at each one and focus on ensuring our ultimate enthusiasm:

Parents

You must forgive your parents, no matter what happened in your life in the past that related to them. The sooner you can fix this and put it behind you, the sooner you can move forward with a happy, successful, productive, and most of all, enthusiastic life.

I dealt with this situation with my own father. My father is a wonderful person today and one of the smartest people I've ever known. One day when I was ten, my mother and father had a terrible argument during my little league game. My father took off ahead of us in another car and we tried to follow as he sped ahead. We drove through a tight suburban residential area, and I noticed my father's car parked sideways in the middle of the street. We pulled up and I jumped out of the car. My father was hovered over a little boy who was lying lifeless in the middle of the road.

The elderly grandmother did not latch the screen door while babysitting her grandson. The boy opened the unsecure door and made his way into the street. My father never saw the errant child and had no time to react.

This was the beginning of the end for my father. This incident led to his battling alcoholism, losing his job, losing his family, and being diagnosed as manic-depressive. My father was never the same after that incident—it led to the problems between my mom and dad until their eventual divorce.

I lost contact with my father during high school. After my second year in the Air Force when I returned from a year of duty being stationed in Turkey, it was time to put this behind me. I found my father and told him that I forgave him for everything in the past. Since that conversation, my father and I have been best friends. I'm thankful I had the conversation with my dad over three decades ago. I recommend for all of you who have a parent who needs to be forgiven: please do it today. Put it behind you, and move forward with your life.

Past intimate relationships
Past marriages or intimate relationships that did not work out can be intense and close to your feelings. They affect your self-worth, and you can become extremely angry and unforgiving toward these people for years.

Remember you were also responsible for any of your past relationships. Have the personal integrity and responsibility to say these words: *I am responsible for this past relationship instead of blaming it on the other person.* Forgive that other person, let him or her go, and say these words: *I forgive him or her for everything, and I wish him or her well.*

Each time you repeat this mantra, the negative emotion attached to this person will begin to decrease. Every time you think of this person, repeat this mantra again: *I forgive him or her for everything and I wish him or her well.*

You will find this is just like turning the heat down on a pot; eventually, this will just go away and you can go on with being enthusiastic.

Everyone who ever hurt you
Friend, boss, crook, and everyone else. Just keep saying, *I forgive them for everything and wish them well.* You will

see as you repeat this mantra every time you think of this person. You will see these feelings gently smolder away.

Go ahead! Forgive yourself!
The last person you must forgive is yourself.

You must forgive yourself for every crazy, ridiculous, silly, stupid mistake that you've made in the past. Stop carrying all these mistakes with you. That was then and this is now. You're not the same person today that you were when you made all those mistakes long ago. If you convict yourself today for mistakes in the past, you would be convicting an innocent man. All of us can look back at things that we did and wonder why about these things. When we made these mistakes, we were younger and less experienced.

We have grown from those past mistakes and moved on. Those mistakes, faults, and indiscriminate decisions are what built us and made us who we are today. You cannot change what happened in the past, you can only move on. Forget about this and again say the mantra, *I forgive myself for every mistake I ever made, I'm a thoroughly good person, and I'm going to have a wonderful future and life.*

Finish the note with *I love myself unconditionally.* Focus on the future and don't worry about the past.

Opportunity Knocks Daily...
Be Grateful and Ignore the
Enthusiasm Killers

Nothing great was ever achieved without enthusiasm.

Ralph Waldo Emerson

What do you do when your enthusiasm doesn't go so well? What about people who don't like seeing your enthusiasm, passion for life, and happiness, and are always shooting down your goals?

Disregard the enthusiasm killers!

You MUST continue moving forward. Enthusiasm and integrating thanks into your life go hand in hand. Look around you; enthusiastic people draw opportunity toward themselves. Opportunity is knocking every day. Answer that door with a smile and attack life with vigor.

I've never seen an unenthusiastic, miserable, unhappy person who was grateful...except for Ebenezer Scrooge—and that took work.

Action

Three 3x5 cards

You know my love of amazing quotes. I keep the quotes below on 3x5 cards, and I carry the cards with me everywhere. There is a reason why enthusiasm was included as the .5 of this book. You can see these quotes fit into every category in the Three Points of Contact.

Pick three quotes you can relate to, such as the ones below. Take three index cards and write one quote on each index card, then carry that index card with you for the next week. Every time an activity that comes up that reminds you of that quote, write it down on the card.

Every production of genius must be the production of enthusiasm.

Benjamin Disraeli

Nothing is so contagious as enthusiasm.

Samuel Taylor Coleridge

You will do foolish things but do them with enthusiasm.

Sidonie Gabrielle Colette

Indeed there is an eloquence in true enthusiasm that cannot be doubted.

Edgar Allan Poe

My strength is my enthusiasm.

Plácido Domingo

The real secret of success is enthusiasm.
Walter Chrysler

It's faith in something and enthusiasm for something that makes life worth living.
Oliver Wendell Holmes, Sr.

A man can succeed at almost anything for which he has unlimited enthusiasm.
Charles Schwab

Enthusiasm is the most important thing in life.
Tennessee Williams

If you have zest and enthusiasm, you attract zest and enthusiasm. Life does not give back in kind.
Norman Vincent Peale

Success consists of going from failure to failure and never losing enthusiasm.
Winston Churchill

Enthusiasm is the greatest asset you can possess, for it can take you further than money, power or influence.
Dada Vaswani

We are always getting ready to live but never living.
Ralph Waldo Emerson

The letter

If you have a relationship that you cannot get over, or you're still feeling bad about a past situation with someone, write a letter and put this behind you. Get a piece of paper, an envelope, and a stamp. You may use electronic media; however, the handwritten note is more personal and extremely sincere.

Write an informal greeting and state, *I forgive you for everything.*

Write down everything you forgive that person for. Write down everything that happened in the past and how they hurt you. You might need several pages for your list—just get it all out so you can move on.

Finish the note with a respectful, *I wish you well.*

Seal the letter and send it off. Whether the person takes the letter in a good or bad way is not the reason for this activity and not your concern. This activity is about freeing yourself.

Once you put that letter in the mail, you are free and you can enjoy yourself and get on with the rest of your life. This is an amazing activity of stress relief and allowing you to move on with all the greatness and success you will achieve.

Key Points

- Daily enthusiasm will get you far!
- Live for today—and live with passion
- Always have a dream for the future
- Forgive and move on from the past
- Opportunity is always knocking…answer!

Beyond the Three Points of Contact

Thanks so much for taking the time to read my book. I hope you are able to find this book helpful in whatever your quests, goals, and dreams that life has in store for you.

What is beyond the Three Points of Contact? You completed the book and have hopefully gone back through the material several times. This book is intended for a life's work and use. You will be able to use these principles throughout your life and hopefully pass them on to friends, family, colleagues, and children.

The world is full of treacherous weather and relentless storms. You will spend your life in and out of arduous weather, and the ability to pull out the rain jacket and umbrella to wait out or punch through the storm is the key. Enjoy! ~ Greg

Don't get overwhelmed

Each chapter has five to eight separate sections and activities at the back of each chapter. You will want to take this slowly and build up momentum. The book is set up in a way that you have the choice of starting from the beginning and working your way through the book chronologically or going directly to a section that appeals to you.

If you pick one chapter from each of the three main points and a section from chapter 12.5, Live Every Day with Enthusiasm, you will be a completely transformed person in one month! If you find this is a bit too much, revisit this book once every two weeks to take a slower approach.

Congratulations! You are now one of the alumni of *Three Points of Contact!* Life's storms better watch out for you. Feel free to contact me directly any time and share your thoughts and experiences.

Gregory Q. Cheek

Author

Appendix

The Community College

"America's Educational Gem"

I'm a proud community college graduate from Shasta College in Redding, California.

I've taught over one hundred community college classes around the world and everywhere in between. If I can fit a class in my schedule, I will teach it. My motto is I will teach "anywhere and anytime." My teaching opportunities include Central Texas College; along the DMZ in South Korea; Barstow College in California's high desert; St. Philip's College in San Antonio, Texas; Community College of Southern Nevada in Las Vegas, Nevada; Kansas Community College at the Federal Military Prison at Ft. Leavenworth; and everywhere else in between. I've turned down more four-year university teaching offers than I've accepted, but I've never turned down an offer to teach at a community college. I will always make room to teach at a community college.

I distinctly remember all my instructors in community college. My Associates of Arts degree (AA) is my most memorable achievement after failing to graduate from high school. The community college is a cornerstone of success and education in the United States.

The open opportunity to attend community college sets the United States apart from any other place in the world. The community college allows anyone the opportunity to attend college and is a wonderful place to knock out the first two years of college at a less expensive rate. Classes generally have a smaller student-to-faculty ratio. Many students get a second chance at a college education or are returning back to college after a break from the dream of pursuing their degree. Community college has a long list of amazing two-year degree, vocational programs, technology programs, and four-year university transfer programs. Many students choose the community college as a smooth transition from high school to a university. Students like having the momentum of an Associate of Arts degree (AA) before transferring to a university.

Overall, the community college is an amazing value. I'm forever grateful to the community college system for giving me the chance as a student and later as a faculty member. Barstow Community College (BCC) gave me my first teaching opportunity in 1997. I taught nights and weekends at Ft. Irwin, California and also received the Faculty of the Year Award from BCC. Teaching is transformational for the students and me. BCC is a typical community college with an amazing faculty, extremely helpful staff, and the most optimistic students anywhere in the world! Barstow College's incredible online education program reaches students from Barstow College and Ft. Irwin to everywhere around the globe. I'm forever grateful for BCC, as I was able to teach my online course while I was going through radiation and chemo in 2010. The ability to teach my students during my cancer treatment is a key reason for my successful recovery, and it helped me stay positive in some very tough times.

Students contact me daily for mentorship after taking my online interpersonal communication class. These students now have bachelor's degrees, MBAs, and PhDs, and are now successful entrepreneurs, pursuing hundreds of professions around the world. However, most of my students clearly recall the interpersonal communication class at BCC. The course connects the textbook, Stephen Covey's *Seven Habits of Highly Effective People*, and insightful interactions among the classroom's fifty students.

My online interpersonal communication course is similar to any community college course I've attended as a student or taught as a faculty member. A large number of community college faculty members have worked in other professions outside of academia. The faculty at Shasta College was comprised of instructors pursuing collegiate teaching as a second or third career. These instructors came with a wealth of professional experience and were intimately involved in assisting with the students' academic goals and dreams.

It's my honor to assist and push success for that first-time college student, returning college student, single parent working multiple jobs, service member deployed around the world, or someone who can only attend a college class virtually. I offer all my students a letter of recommendation to assist with their networking portfolio. My students can contact me anytime if they need assistance or a mentor for as long as I'm capable. Never too early to start networking!

The community college agreement of support is forever, and the lineage is long and caring! This is a strong fraternity of sharing knowledge and assisting the next generation of community college graduates. Notable community college graduates include George Lucas, Tom Hanks, Walt Disney, Halle Barry, Eddie Murphy,

Billy Crystal, Clint Eastwood, Nolan Ryan, Ross Perot, Sarah Palin, James Belushi, Aaron Rodgers, and George Brett.

Of all the motivational presentations I've delivered around the world, my most memorable are those to the faculty and students at community colleges across America. I present one-hour to multiple-day presentations at universities around the world. However, I have a warm place in my heart—and I always will—for the community colleges and our amazing faculty, staff, and students!

Acknowledgements

To my remarkable medical team: Dr. Lisa Shnayder, Dr. Pravesh Kumar, Dr. Prakash Neupani, Dr. Leonard Lousten, Mary Moody, Vicki Liston, and the entire staff at the University of Kansas Cancer Center, Dental Associates, and the University of Kansas Head and Neck Cancer Support Group. We did it—I'm forever thankful!

To Mary Cheek: Thank you for being such an amazing mother to our children. They are extremely successful because of your dedication, love, and support. I would not have made it out of Shasta College without you.

To Ani Cheek, for your endearing love and support of this book.

To my father Gerald Cheek: Thank you for the best advice ever on my eighteenth birthday. "Go find your way in life." It was not easy, but I did it! Your life was far from easy and I'm thankful for our friendship over the past thirty years.

I'm forever grateful to the Seattle Pacific University Women's Volleyball Program for your prayers and faith in my recovery.

To C Team, Mission Command Training Program (MCTP) at Ft. Leavenworth, Kansas for the support of year one cancer-free from May 10, 2010 to Aug 1, 2011. European Command

Headquarters, Stuttgart, Germany, J5-Plans: Thanks for your support from year one to year five. This journey beyond cancer might not be possible without either of these great teams and organizations. You are both family, and I'm forever grateful.

To my thousands of Greg Cheek communication college course alumni students around the world—you are my inspiration!

I would need an entire book to thank everyone for the life's journey in which I wrote this book. Thanks to all my family members, friends, and colleagues around the world for your endearing support and inspiration. To everyone I've met around the world, I look forward to catching up when we see each other again.

As they say in Germany, *Auf Wiedersehen* (until
me meet again)!

Go get 'em and always maintain

Three Points of Contact

Greg

About the Author

Gregory Q. Cheek is an author, college professor, motivational speaker and owner of Greg Cheek Speaks LLC. Greg presents an array of motivational topics, including keynote presentations, overcoming adversity and achieving your dreams, goal setting, dealing with cancer and illness, resiliency, collegiate faculty communication, healthcare communication between patient and provider, presentation training and overcoming speaker apprehension, leadership communication, and athlete and team confidence through effective communication, and the Three Points of Contact and his 12.5 Ways of Success.

Greg holds an Associate of Arts (AA) degree from Shasta College, a Bachelor of Arts (BA) degree from California State University, Chico, and a Master of Arts (MA) degree in Communication from the University of Northern Colorado. Greg is a Distinguished Military Graduate from the Reserve Officer Training Corps, a graduate of the US Army Command and General Staff College, and a graduate of the Master Resiliency Training (MRT) at the University of Pennsylvania.

Greg served six years in the US Air Force as an airman and sixteen years as an officer in the United States Army. Greg was awarded an Air Medal when the helicopter he was traveling on was forced to conduct an emergency landing in enemy territory during combat operations. Greg is a recipient of the US Army Douglas MacArthur Leadership Award and has served in leadership roles in the First Infantry Division, Ft. Riley, Kansas, Second Infantry Division, Korea, and Fourth Infantry Division, Ft. Carson, Colorado, and as a General Officer Aide de Camp during Operation Desert Shield and Desert Storm.

Greg has taught more than a hundred college communication courses around the world and served on faculty at the US Army Combined Armed Services Staff College (CAS3), the US Army Command and General Staff College, the US Army Medical Department Center and School (AMEDD), University of Nevada, Las Vegas, St. Mary's University, University of Maryland University College in Germany, University of Kansas, St. Philip's College, Community College of Southern Nevada, Barstow College, Kansas City Kansas Community College, and Central Texas College in South Korea.

Greg's passions are travel, motivational speaking, communication seminars, healthcare communication, and collegiate communication and teaching communication at the college and university level. Greg's motto is to "speak anywhere and anytime." Greg has delighted audiences in more than twenty countries worldwide.

**Feel the Power
of the
Three Points of Contact
in Person!**

*Find out more
about bringing
Greg
to your organization at the
contact information below.*

www.gregcheekspeaks.com
greg@gregcheekspeaks.com

CPSIA information can be obtained at www.ICGtesting.com
Printed in the USA
LVOW11s1956271015

459954LV00006B/567/P